KU-203-074

Contents

1

The world of sport and leisure

What do we mean by ...?

For most people, life is divided crudely into two parts: work and free time. A recent survey shows that, on average, the working population of the UK spend only 25 per cent of their time at work; 27 per cent is spent asleep and 20 per cent on essential activities such as eating, housework and caring for children. This means that nearly 30 per cent of time is available for people to spend as they wish. Much of this **free time** is taken up by what is referred to as **leisure**. There is a tendency to think of leisure as time when we do little or nothing. That is wrong, for the essence of leisure is doing those things we choose to do. Such activities provide various benefits, such as pleasure and satisfaction, entertainment and improved knowledge, and amusement and relaxation. They would include what are often referred to as **hobbies**. These leisure-time activities, particularly those pursued outside the home, are normally referred to as **recreation**. So as **1.1** indicates, whilst most leisure is devoted to recreation, there are still those times of relative inactivity when we just potter around the house, relax in the garden or watch TV.

Figure 1.1 The relationships between leisure, recreation, sport and tourism in free time

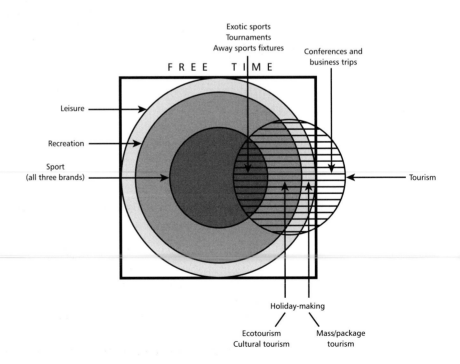

So **leisure** is about personal choice and doing in our free time those things that give us pleasure and satisfaction. It can involve any combination of an immense range of diverse activities, from sleeping in and skate-boarding to clubbing and chatting on-line. For many of us, leisure is being with family and friends, travelling, gardening or perhaps browsing in fashion stores. No doubt you have your own ideas about leisure. But the point is this. No matter what might turn us 'on', leisure is inherently therapeutic. It has immense potential to improve our welfare, our quality of life and our general sense of well-being. The common distinction between home-based leisure and that undertaken outside the home is noteworthy (**1.2**). The latter activities are perhaps of more interest in geographical study, with its focus on spatial location and movement.

Figure 1.2 Leisure activities

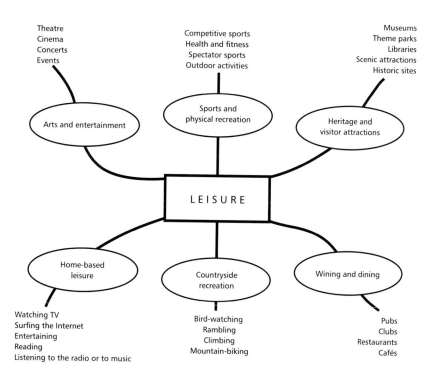

When we look more closely at the recreational component of leisure, we find that **sport** is increasingly significant and popular, particularly in MEDCs. This results from:

- an increasing amount of leisure time to fill
- a growing love of competitive activities
- the promotion of sport through the media
- the emergence of sport as business
- a mounting concern about personal health and welfare.

John Bale (2000), a leading sports geographer, has pointed out that it is difficult to define the word 'sport': 'It can be used to define almost any activity ranging from darts to dancing, from chess to cricket, from fishing to football.' A number of distinctions are commonly drawn, as for example between 'competitive' and 'non-competitive', 'spectator' and 'non-spectator', and 'outdoor' and 'indoor' sports. Bale, however, suggests that instead we should recognise three different forms or brands (**1.3**):

- **play sport** – done for fun and often spontaneously (a game of beach cricket, or hill-walking)
- **welfare sport** – undertaken in order to keep fit and healthy (for example, jogging or time in a fitness gym)
- **achievement sport** – a deadly serious and highly competitive business, in which people and teams seek to prove their superiority (for example, athletics or league football).

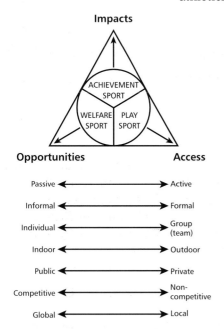

Figure 1.3 Three forms of sport and their associated spectra

It needs to be stressed that most individual sports can be undertaken in these three different forms (**1.3**). Take golf, for example. There are many who play it just for fun and relaxation. There are others who play it in the belief that the exercise involved is good for their health. There are still others – the 'professionals' – who play 'for real' in order to make their name and earn a living. But even when golf is played for fun or health, a competitive element may be evident, simply because most players cannot resist trying to either lower their own scores or underscore others. Indeed, a competitive element may even be detected in seemingly non-competitive sports such as hill-walking and mountaineering. What are hill-walkers and mountaineers doing other than pitching their fitness and nerve against Nature's peaks and precipices?

What begins to emerge here is the idea of a sports spectrum ranging from 'for fun' to 'for real' (that is, for money or better health). If you push this idea a little further, you come to realise that there is not one view, but a number of different spectra running across sport as a whole (**1.3**). Some of them were indicated earlier. It is more than likely that the same spectra can be detected in many leisure activities. Similarly, the three key dimensions of sport – namely opportunity, access and impact (on people and places) – also apply to leisure.

For the purposes of this book, the term **sport** is confined to those free-time activities that are overtly competitive, organised and largely to do with achievement. Much of this calibre of sport is increasingly big business. Just think of the huge sums of money involved today in football transfers and in the sponsorship of Formula 1 motor racing. Our possible involvement in such sport may be as both participant and spectator. At the same time, we might see all those other brands of sport (the non-competitive, the impromptu, the relaxed, the health-driven, etc.) as yet another component of leisure.

The relationships between the four concepts just considered (free time, leisure, recreation and sport) are shown in **1.1**. Leisure is represented as a subset of free time, recreation as a subset of leisure and sport as a subset of recreation. However, cutting across all four is **tourism**, a term used to cover

THE GEOGRAPHY
OF SPORT AND
LEISURE

Sue Warn and
Michael Witherick

Series editor
Michael Witherick

Published in 2003 by:
Nelson Thornes Ltd
Delta Place
27 Bath Road
CHELTENHAM
GL53 7TH
United Kingdom

03 04 05 06 07 / 10 9 8 7 6 5 4 3 2 1

A catalogue record for this book is available from the British Library

ISBN 0 7487 7408 4

Illustrations by DC Graphic Design Ltd and Angela Lumley
Page make-up by DC Graphic Design Ltd
Printed and bound in Great Britian by Ashford Colour Press

This book is dedicated to Professor John Bale.

Acknowledgements
The authors and publishers are grateful to the following for permission to
reproduce photographs and other copyright material in this book:

Geographical Association/J Bale, fig 4.1; GeoNews Review, fig 2.8; The *Guardian,*
fig 5.7; Heinemann, fig 1.5; D. Mountjoy, fig 2.1; Spon Press, fig 1.4; US
Orienteering Federation, fig 3.7; www.mintel.co.uk, fig 6.3; J Wipperman (King
Edward VI Grammar School, Chelmsford) fig 5.9; Yew Consulting (& Stoke on
Trent Sixth Form College), fig 3.12.

Corel 487(NT), fig 5.6; getmapping plc, fig 2.5; PA Photos, figs 2.10, 4.2, 4.3, 4.6,
5.4; Photodisc 67 (NT), fig 3.6.

The publishers apologise to anyone whose rights have been inadvertently
overlooked and will be happy to rectify any errors or omissions.

Lycra® is a registered trademark of the Du Pont Corporation.

all those activities undertaken by people when staying away from home for at least one night. So this includes holiday-making, staying with friends and relatives and involvement in 'away' sports fixtures, as well as attending conferences and business meetings. Tourism is explored in another book in this EPICS series (see Warn, 1999). The leisure in focus in this book is largely of an everyday nature, local to home and of short duration. Within that focus, the spotlight falls particularly on sport of all kinds.

Review

1 Undertake a stratified survey among your fellow students to establish:

- their top leisure activities
- an estimate of the percentage of their leisure time devoted to sport.

Is there a strong consensus? Are there noticeable gender differences?

SECTION B

Sport and leisure – an industry?

Reference is often made these days to the 'sport and leisure industry'. You might be thinking 'Is there not something of a contradiction here?' Industry is about the world of work, surely, while sport and leisure are, for most of us, about free time (**1.1**)! The answer to this apparent dichotomy lies in the fact that most forms of sport and much leisure activity require the production of goods and the provision of services. So the sport and leisure industry is to be seen as encompassing three main components:

- the activities themselves – for example, going swimming, listening to music, and clubbing
- the products associated with sport and leisure – for example, videos and CDs, sports shoes and clothing
- the leisure services – for example, leisure centres, fitness clubs, cinemas and stadiums.

What we might begin to see are demand and supply situations within both the secondary and tertiary sectors of the economy.

Let us follow through the sequence of demands set in motion by just one leisure-cum-sport development: the setting up of a private fitness club in a town (see case study in **Chapter 3 Section C**). The simplified sequence portrayed may be set out as follows:

- market research
- acquisition of site and planning permission
- construction of new premises or conversion of existing building
- installation of fitness equipment
- staff training
- advertising and recruitment of members
- day-to-day running of the club.

Each of these simplified stages requires the input of resources. They range from land and building materials to specialist equipment. At all stages, there is a changing demand for labour. When the club is up and running, there will be a constant need for personal trainers and regular maintenance of the equipment. Club members will need to buy appropriate clothing equipment, such as trainers and tracksuits. No doubt, these goods will have been manufactured in and imported from some LEDC. At all times, there will be a careful monitoring of income and expenditure, for at the end of the day no club is going to survive if the former is exceeded by the latter.

Figure 1.4 The sports business

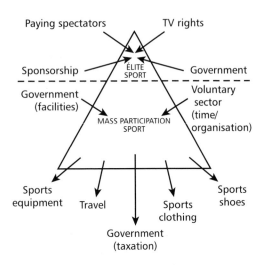

The possible image of sport as business is perhaps reinforced by the connections and links shown in **1.4**. At the élite sport apex of the triangle, there are huge capital flows in the form of entrance fees, sponsorship and government support. At the populist base of the triangle, some very obvious commercial links are shown, most of them to do with sporting gear.

The production of goods and the provision of services represent the business or provider part of leisure. This is the supply side. Technology, economics and fashion are among the factors that influence it (**1.5**). The other major part of the system is the demand or consumer side. Our consumption of leisure goods and services is conditioned by many things: what we do for a living, how much we earn, how much spare time we have, and whether or not our gender, social class or ethnicity prevent us from having proper access to leisure opportunities.

It is hoped that enough has been said to convince you that there is a clear economic dimension to much sport and leisure. Sport and leisure provide a livelihood for an increasing number of people. In many MEDCs, leisure has become a major source of employment and a favourite target for investment.

Figure 1.5 The leisure system

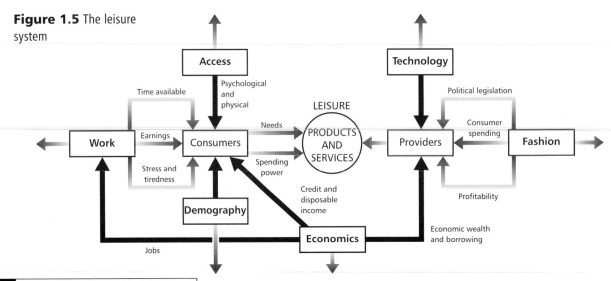

Review

2 Draw a diagram to represent the sequence involved in setting up the private fitness club. At each stage, identify the specific inputs.

3 Study **1.5** and check that you understand and can illustrate the arrow links shown in the diagram.

SECTION C

Where's the geography?

The geography of sport and leisure becomes apparent when we apply four key ideas of modern geography. They are the interlinked concepts of space, place, environment and scale. All that needs to be done here is briefly to remind you what each concept is about and to give the flavour of what is involved in the contexts of sport and leisure. They provide a framework that will be fleshed out and illustrated in subsequent chapters.

Space

Space in geography means the surface of the Earth and its use by people. Since all leisure requires space, it is therefore a user of space. The demand for leisure space may range from the desktop occupied by your PC at home to vast tracts of open countryside or wilderness. In between, we might note such recreational spaces as gardens and parks, cinemas and camp-sites, lakes and beaches. Many sports have very specific space requirements. Think of:

- the 22 yard (20.12 m) wicket in cricket and the necessary outfield
- the ordered space of the football pitch, with its 12 yards (11 m) between the goal line and the penalty spot
- the 78 foot (23.77 m) length of the tennis court
- the 400 m long oval of the athletics track
- the spaced 18 holes of the golf course.

Less prescriptive, but no less important, are the space needs of sports stadiums in general, skiing, sailing, climbing and orienteering, to name but a few activities.

Place

Place in geography is about the uniqueness and distinctiveness of different parts of the Earth's surface. With leisure, place is significant in that it can affect what people do in their free time. Just as the notion of leisure varies from person to person, so it does from place to place (see **Chapter 3**). For example, because of climatic considerations, leisure during the winter months in high latitudes tends to be home-based and undertaken indoors. Culture too is likely to have a bearing, in the sense that tradition and custom will favour certain forms of recreation over others. In Islamic countries, for example, tradition still decrees that a woman's place is the home. This clearly impacts on what might be done during leisure time. In many LEDCs, the pressures of survival severely restrict leisure time and recreational opportunities (see **Chapter 2**). Not only are rates of participation going to be less than in the North, but the forms it takes are also likely to be different. This point is illustrated by the sport and leisure profiles of six people living in different parts of the world (**1.6**).

In achievement sport, place assumes a particular importance. Much serious sport is representational, with individuals and teams seen as 'symbolising' places. Those places may be schools and universities, towns and cities, or counties and countries. Almost all sports teams are named after places. For example, just look at the names of teams in English football leagues or in the US baseball league. Similarly, almost all the top-flight men and women in individual sports, such as athletics, tennis and golf, are seen as personifying the places they come from.

Figure 1.6 Sport and leisure portraits from around the world

Isatou Bamaku, aged 12, from Malawi

Nearly all my time is taken up by looking after our cattle and having to collect firewood and water for the family. My parents paid for me to go to school until I was 11. At school, because I was tall for my age, I was good at netball. I was chosen to play for a youth team, but my parents couldn't afford the kit or the cost of travelling to matches. There's not much to do here after dark except to cook and talk with others living in the family compound. Maybe one day we will have a TV set!

Senzo Nakamura, aged 43, from Japan

My main sport used to be the martial arts, but now I spend more time on my mountain bike, cycling with my wife and our son around the local parks. Now and again I do some weight-training at a local gym. I would love to play golf, but can't afford it. I also like going round museums and visiting interesting places, but leisure time is very limited. My other main leisure activity is surfing – on the Internet, not the beach!

Juan Sebastian, aged 17, from Argentina

Before the economic 'crash' I did all sorts of sport, as my mother had a good job in the local leisure centre. I also used to ride and sometimes play polo. The centre is now shut and we have been forced to leave our home near the centre of Buenos Aires and move into a two-roomed shanty dwelling on the outskirts. Here I manage to play a bit of football with the lads in the alley, but much of my time is spent doing odd jobs to get a bit of extra cash. I'm still at school and we do sport there.

Renata Miller, aged 51, from California

My husband is a oil company executive, so I don't have to work. We decided not to have any kids. I do several hours a week helping in the local charity shop, and spend a lot of time trying to keep fit and healthy. I have my own personal trainer for four hours a week, and I work out in a gym and swim every morning. Most days I also jog along the beach. Twice a week I go to t'ai chi. This is a wonderful part of the world to live in; the only problem is that it is so sunny. This ages the skin – so I need regular beauty therapy.

Jamila Khan, aged 30, from Bangladesh

Having five kids aged between five and 12, I'm not really sure what leisure is. I'm kept very busy looking after and feeding them. My husband is not paid well, so I am now working in a co-operative making jute bags. It was set up two years ago with a loan from the bank. When I can find time, I am learning to write and do sums, so that I can help more with the running of the co-operative. We don't have any sports facilities in the village, but some of the boys swim in the river. The girls spend their time learning to sew and make carpets.

Erik Olsen, aged 62, from Norway

Although I am now retired, my hobbies are still outdoors. For most of the year, I fish in the fjord. I continue to do some cross-country skiing in the winter. In the summer, when there's 24 hours of daylight, my wife and I prefer to stay in the log cabin that I built over 25 years ago down by the shore. I enjoy walking along the beach. On calm evenings I will row the boat out and just watch the sun go nearly down. My three children have all left home, but they still love all sorts of sport, thanks to the great opportunities they had at the local school.

Environment

Environment has a two-way focus in geography. It looks at the impact that the natural world has on human activities and the reciprocal impact of people on that world. The natural environment is to be seen as offering resources (opportunities) that are there to be exploited by sport and other leisure activities. Winter snow is one such resource of widespread significance in MEDCs. Hot springs are another, but they are more localised: outside Japan and Iceland, they remain little exploited in the context of leisure. The environmental resources of LEDCs are perhaps more to do with sun, sea and wildlife.

The issue of environmental impact is one that increasingly confronts us, whether it is that of a proposed airport extension or the opening up of a new oilfield. But the potential impacts of sport and leisure are no less serious (see **Chapter 4**). Think of the impact that sports stadiums of all kinds and the crowds they draw have on adjacent residential areas and their inhabitants. Think too of the footpath erosion and trampling that are now scarring so many national parks, simply because too many people wish to spend some of their leisure time in these protected areas. Think of the environmental costs of converting farmland and countryside into golf courses.

Scale

The above concepts may all be pursued at a range of different spatial scales, running from local to global, through regional and national. Some of those scale differences have been implied under the three previous headings. Perhaps all that needs to be added and stressed at this stage is the 'localness' of much leisure activity. Most of our leisure time is spent at or close to home. In contrast, professional or achievement sport shows increasingly the hallmarks of globalisation (see **Chapter 5**). The symptoms include:

- the international movements of sports-players – such as to the chosen clubs of the top-flight footballers
- the organisation of global sports series – as in tennis, golf and motor racing
- the holding of regular global tournaments – such as the Olympic Games and the World Cup
- the global marketing of sports goods manufacturers – such as by Nike, Adidas and Puma.

So that sets out the four basic concepts that underlie the geography of sport and leisure. It is now up to the next five chapters to explain and exemplify that geography.

Review

4 'When it comes to leisure space, water is as important as land.' Explain and exemplify.

5 Can you think of any more resources of the natural environment that are exploited by leisure activities?

6 What might you expect to come into focus at the regional scale in a geographical view of sport and leisure?

7 What conclusions about sport and leisure do you draw from the six portraits in 1.6?

Enquiry

Look at the list of 100 companies involved in the FTSE Index today. How many would you recognise as part of the sport and leisure industry?

CHAPTER 2

Sport, leisure and development

Many believe that the global sport and leisure industry is currently growing at an exponential rate, fuelled by increased leisure time and the personal affluence that come with economic development. The reality is much more complex for, as indicated in **Chapter 1**, the sport and leisure industry is multifaceted (see **1.2** on page 5). Furthermore, because it depends on consumers, it is highly volatile and its fortunes are closely linked to an ever-changing economic climate. As a country becomes more developed economically, levels of investment in the industry and the depth of sporting ability increase. Equally, improvements to sport and leisure facilities can invigorate both regional and national economies. Thus a two-way symbiotic relationship possibly exists between economic development and sport and leisure (**2.1**).

Figure 2.1 A model of sport and leisure development, based on Rostow's model of economic development

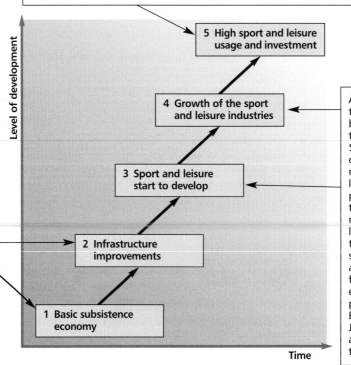

The most economically developed countries, the prosperous 'North', are at stage **5** of the model. They have high investment, uptake and ability in a number of sports, resulting in success in international competitions. The citizens have more free time and more disposable income, so they can afford to spend more on sport and leisure. These countries still bid to host global events to confirm their place in the world, and are more successful due to their already developed infrastructure. A major event can still have large positive effects at both local and national scales.

In the early stages of development, there will be very little sport and leisure. At first, the economy is based on subsistence agriculture and a very strong primary sector. Gradually, as the economy moves into stage **2**, the infrastructure will start to develop, but there are higher priorities for investment than sport and leisure – healthcare and education, for example.

Level of development

5 High sport and leisure usage and investment

4 Growth of the sport and leisure industries

3 Sport and leisure start to develop

2 Infrastructure improvements

1 Basic subsistence economy

Time

As countries develop further, sport and leisure begin to develop. It is at the crucial GDP level of $1000 per capita that consumers begin to spend money on sport and leisure – when this happens, investment in these things will increase dramatically (illustrated by the large growth in Asian theme parks), and so will sporting ability. Countries at this level also start to bid for international sporting events, in order to gain a place on the world stage. Examples of this are the Japanese, South Korean and Chinese Olympics, and the Malaysian Grand Prix.

The anatomy of the world's fastest growing industry

The rapid expansion of the sport and leisure industry is evidenced in different ways, as for example in rising participation rates, diversifying activities and products, and in the provision of more and better facilities. A number of factors have contributed to this take-off (**2.2**).

Figure 2.2 A mind map of factors leading to dynamism in the sport and leisure industry

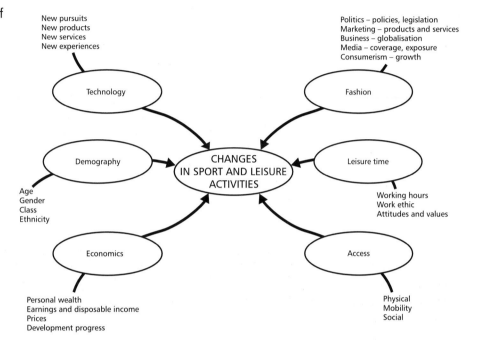

New pursuits
New products
New services
New experiences

Politics – policies, legislation
Marketing – products and services
Business – globalisation
Media – coverage, exposure
Consumerism – growth

Technology

Fashion

Demography

CHANGES IN SPORT AND LEISURE ACTIVITIES

Leisure time

Age
Gender
Class
Ethnicity

Working hours
Work ethic
Attitudes and values

Economics

Access

Personal wealth
Earnings and disposable income
Prices
Development progress

Physical
Mobility
Social

Leisure time

This has already been defined in **Chapter 1 Section A**. As countries develop economically, technological developments, such as automation, are supposed to lead to decreasing working hours and the emergence of a leisured society (**2.2**). This is true for many MEDCs, such as France, where working weeks of 30–33 hours are a reality. The paradox is, however, that in other countries, such as the UK, the USA and Japan, whilst leisure consumption has been rising, leisure time for the employed has actually declined. This trend is counterbalanced by ageing societies in which over 20 per cent of the people are retired and, as such, now form a significant leisure market. In addition, the 8–10 per cent who are unemployed in many of those societies also form a niche market with lots of leisure time but limited money. For today's mainstream market, sport and leisure activities need to be accessible in terms of both time and place. Short, sharp and flexible activities, such as fitness gyms and short breaks to neighbouring countries by low-cost airlines, are currently in vogue.

	1990	1995
	(000s)	(000s)
Football	2350	1650
Golf	1002	1217
Squash	513	465
Sailing	300	450
Rugby Union	297	284
Lawn tennis	250	275
Swimming	217	280
Athletics	261	248
Martial arts	99	177
Badminton	101	84
Total	5390	5130

Figure 2.3 Changes in the membership of UK sports clubs, 1990–1995

Figure 2.4 Changes in the percentage participating in sport and leisure in the UK, 1986–2001

	1986		2001	
	Males	Females	Males	Females
Watching TV	97	97	99	99
Gardening	54	58	40	48
Jogging	10	6	17	14
Walking	41	49	36	46
Snooker/billiards	26	18	5	3
Cycling	10	15	7	8
Swimming	14	13	15	19
Darts	14	11	3	3
Soccer	10	1	8	4
Golf	6	2	8	3
Martial arts	2	1	4	3
Aerobics, dance and gymnastics	6	8	12	18

Fashion

In an industry that is increasingly controlled by large national and multinational companies (TNCs), such as Fitness First and Rank, standardised products have begun to dominate the world of sport and leisure (**2.2**). Extensive media coverage and their associated commercial advertising are reinforcing the trend. There are now over 300 major sport and leisure magazines worldwide, and hundreds of dedicated sport and leisure TV channels. Marketing analyses patterns of consumer behaviour; it reinforces consumerism and encourages spending on the latest lifestyle activity, equipment and clothes. Governments can also play a role in promoting sport and leisure, as for example through the UK's Sport for All campaign (see **3.4** on page 32). Legislation can encourage developments, as for example by extending the licensing hours for pubs and clubs, or easing planning regulations that might otherwise constrain the siting and design of new sports stadiums. Fashion generates rapid changes in the popularity of activities. Figures **2.3** and **2.4** show how patterns of sport and leisure in the UK have changed over a short period.

Access

Access has a number of different connotations (**2.2**):

- **Physical access** – this depends on the availability and provision of quality facilities, such as new sports halls, pools and all-weather surfaces.
- **Mobility access** – whilst 80 per cent of people in the UK travel to sport and leisure activities by car, the lack of public transport can be critical for both the young and the elderly, and in remote rural areas. Access for the disabled is a further issue that only government legislation can overcome. One particular sticking-point here is the cost of installing lifts, ramps and other special equipment in old-fashioned facilities.
- **Social access** – initially, many sport activities were élitist. People were excluded from participation by high costs (for example, golf club membership fees) and social class (for example, tennis was very much a middle-class preserve). More recently, sport in the UK has proved to be ethnically divisive. This was evidenced by the dearth of British-born Black players in county cricket, and by the abuse directed at Black players in league soccer. Even today, there are groups who perceive that they are excluded from some sports. Certainly, there are still barriers to participation that need to be removed.

Economics

Economics plays a very important role, both nationally and at regional and local scales (**2.2**). The sport and leisure industry, particularly with regard to spectator sports, is very sensitive to levels of wealth and disposable income. In times of hardship, these are the first areas to be 'trimmed back'. Equally, the state of the national economy determines the amount of public money available for spending on sport and leisure projects.

The health of the sport and leisure industry is vital to both national and regional economies. In the UK, for example:

- consumer spending on sport-related goods and services was estimated to be nearly £12 billion in 1995 and is forecast to double by 2005
- the value added to the UK economy by sport-related activity was nearly £10 billion in 1995
- employment in sport-related activities currently stands at half a million jobs, but 40 per cent of these are part-time.

Demography

Current demographic trends suggest that the UK, like other MEDCs, is a 'greying' society (**2.2**). This is affecting the nature of sport and leisure provision as well as the profile of participation rates. Sport is even being prescribed for health reasons under some NHS plans for care of the elderly. Despite recent fears about failing pensions, early retirement among middle-class professionals continues to release 'grey pounds' that are spent mainly on leisure. Equally, the latest Census (2001) revealed a high percentage of single people in the adult population. They, in their turn, appear to be creating a demand for particular types of sport and leisure opportunities, such as clubs, gyms and bars. The 'pink pounds' of the gay community are part of this growing market. In general, there is a gender split in sport and leisure, with women showing lower participation in sport but higher participation in leisure. The Census also revealed the UK, like many other European countries, to be an increasingly multi-ethnic society. Traditionally, some ethnic groups have shown lower participation rates in sport than others. For example, the participation rate for people of Pakistani ethnic origin in the UK is 37 per cent, as compared with 70 per cent for the Chinese community and 65 per cent for Whites. On the other hand, this multi-ethnicity has helped to diversify leisure developments, such as the current Bollywood cinema boom, yoga and the martial arts.

Technology

Technology has a very important impact on the design of products and services (**2.2**). Notable here is the huge emphasis on performance. This has led to revolutionary developments such as the introduction of graphite frames for tennis racquets, advances in the design of sports shoes and the use of new fabrics such as Lycra® and neoprene in sportswear. Advertising and marketing, using famous sporting stars as models, persuade people to buy the latest gear in the hope that they might become a David Beckham, a Tiger Woods or a Michael Jordan. New technology also creates new extreme leisure

Review

1 Attempt to rank the above six factors in terms of their contribution to the take-off in the UK sport and leisure industry.

2 Study **2.3** and **2.4**.
- Analyse the changes shown.
- Research the reasons for the changes.

experiences, such as the 'X sports' available at Queenstown (New Zealand), the 'extreme sport capital' of the world. New technology can also reduce costs, as for example via silicon chips in computer technology, or in new materials such as the fibreglass used in the manufacture of the new long surfboard.

Sport and the economic development process

Since the 1980s, MEDC governments have increasingly seen a role for culture, sport, leisure and tourism in the promotion of economic development, particularly in the regeneration of urban and even remote rural areas. The catalyst was the substantial collapse in manufacturing employment, particularly in the 1970s and early 1980s. This **deindustrialisation** resulted from the global shift of production from MEDCs towards lower-cost centres in NICs and RICs. At the same time, there was a migration of the remaining production within large urban areas, from cramped inner-city premises to more attractive urban fringe and green-field sites. As a consequence, industrial cities suffered severe job losses. For example, between 1971 and 1980 Birmingham lost 190 000 jobs, Sheffield 60 000 and East Manchester 50 000. Unemployment rates often rose to 20 per cent among skilled adult males. Had the situation been left to market forces, there would have been absolutely no chance of these severely deprived and depressed areas ever recovering. Their poor image and infrastructure would have precluded them from attracting either new businesses or people with the necessary new-era labour skills.

Whilst regional development policies have been very successful in attracting new high-tech manufacturing to areas such as South Wales and the new towns, attracting new types of manufacturing industry back into inner cities has proved to be nigh on impossible. It has been discovered that considerable investments in infrastructure and facilities have to be made before any new revitalising activities might be attracted in. Initially, city authorities pinned their hopes on attracting service industries, but more recently it has been recognised that sport and leisure may well have a particular role to play in this economic recovery. The transitional zones of many CBDs contain some outstanding, often listed, buildings, such as old railways stations, defunct power stations and abandoned warehouses. These are crying out for new uses. The housing of the Tate Modern Gallery in a disused power station and the conversion of the site of a derelict gas works in Manchester into a world-class velodrome for cycling are just two examples of what can be done. Brown-field sites abound in inner-city areas; they offer relatively cheap land and often good access.

Sport is just one of a number of sectors that has the potential to activate urban regeneration. Culture and tourism are two others. Leeds has opted for culture, whilst Liverpool and Newcastle (with Gateshead) have put in powerful bids for European City of Culture status in 2003. Other cities, such as Bradford, have looked more to tourism as a focus for regeneration.

In contrast, Manchester (see case study on page 19) and Sheffield have opted for sport as the main thrust. Sport has already proved to be particularly effective when working alongside other closely related sectors. In Birmingham and London, for example, sport is just one part of a multi-strand approach that also involves the arts, culture and tourism. The National Indoor Arena and the long-awaited new Wembley Stadium will be capable of accommodating a huge variety of events.

Case study: New sports facilities and the regeneration of Sheffield

During the 1970s and 1980s, Sheffield suffered a serious economic recession as its coal, steel and engineering industries declined. The loss of jobs amounted to over 60 000 and in parts of the city the unemployment rate reached 20 per cent. With little hope of any help from government, the city decided that one possible path to recovery was to follow an event-led tourism strategy. The first major step was achieved in 1991 when the city hosted the World Student Games. An investment of £150 million was made in new sports facilities, including an athletics stadium (**2.5**), an indoor arena and an international-standard swimming pool.

The World Student Games itself made an operating loss of £10 million, but no account was taken of the economic activity generated by visitors who came to watch or participate in the event. However, the investment in infrastructure has borne fruit, because since 1991 over 300 sports events have been held in Sheffield, including part of the European Cup soccer tournament in 1996. So far, additional expenditure in the local economy generated by visitors associated with these events has amounted to an estimated £30 million.

Figure 2.5 The World Student Games stadium – a catalyst of Sheffield's revival

Thanks to the brave decision made some 15 years ago, Sheffield has successfully shaken off the image of a dirty industrial city. Along with Birmingham and Glasgow, it is now designated a 'national city of sport'. But the benefits spread further than that, for the city has experienced an upturn in its fortunes as a business and service centre. Investments have been made in the improvement of the urban fabric and the transport system.

The sorts of developments just mentioned rely heavily on public finance. In some circumstances, it has proved possible to attract substantial private funding. The formation of a partnership between the public and private sectors seems to be a prerequisite if a city bids to host a major sporting event, such as the Olympic or Commonwealth Games. Bidding is further strengthened if there is central government backing. Currently, this is most likely to be achieved if a proposed sport or leisure development can be linked to the economic regeneration of an area – a top government priority.

Figure 2.6 Myrdal's model of cumulative causation applied to sport and leisure

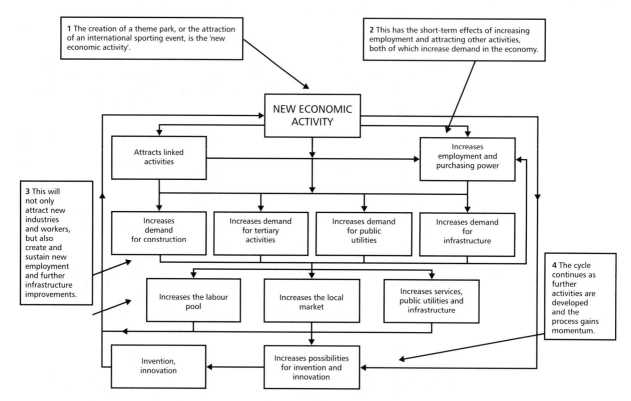

1 The creation of a theme park, or the attraction of an international sporting event, is the 'new economic activity'.

2 This has the short-term effects of increasing employment and attracting other activities, both of which increase demand in the economy.

NEW ECONOMIC ACTIVITY

Attracts linked activities

Increases employment and purchasing power

3 This will not only attract new industries and workers, but also create and sustain new employment and further infrastructure improvements.

Increases demand for construction

Increases demand for tertiary activities

Increases demand for public utilities

Increases demand for infrastructure

4 The cycle continues as further activities are developed and the process gains momentum.

Increases the labour pool

Increases the local market

Increases services, public utilities and infrastructure

Invention, innovation

Increases possibilities for invention and innovation

In the **short term,** major sporting and leisure events create direct employment. However, innovative strategies need to be developed if this employment is to be sustained and a boost given to the local sport and leisure economy. One course of action is to ensure year-round use of the facilities after the festival or event, mainly by the local community. In the **longer term,** these events and their facilities can help to attract further investment, as well as **re-image** the city, region or even country in the contexts of tourism and business. What has been set in train, as illustrated by Sheffield (see page 17) and Manchester (see page 19), is a process of cumulative causation (**2.6**). It is claimed that economic regeneration is usually paralleled by **social** regeneration, with the improved image creating a feel-good factor locally and even nationally. Depending on their nature, these events can also provide previously disadvantaged populations with excellent sport and leisure facilities and encourage higher rates of participation.

The typology shown in **2.7** aims to clarify the links between major sport and leisure events and economic development.

Figure 2.7 A typology of sport and leisure events

TYPE A

Irregular, one-off global or major international spectator events, lasting for a considerable period. If managed properly, these events have the potential to generate significant economic activity and media interest, and thus have large revenue-raising potential via TV rights and sponsorship, in addition to direct spectator sales.

Examples include the Olympics, World Cup soccer, the European Cup football championships, the Ryder Cup and the Commonwealth Games. It is likely that the World Athletics Championships might join this.

Note that these events usually have to be bid for, often at huge expense.

TYPE B

Major spectator sports events, generating significant economic activity and media interest, that form part of an annual cycle of sports events; such as Six Nations rugby, Test Match cricket, Open golf, ATP tennis tournaments, and both Formula 1 and IAAF Grand Prix circuits. Overall, at a global scale the UK is fortunate in being over-represented in these events.

In many cases these events go to fixed locations, and so represent a lower-risk investment (predictable spectator markets and media coverage). Existing centres fight very hard to hang on to their places on the circuit; for example, Silverstone was threatened with the loss of the British Grand Prix because of car parking and traffic congestion problems.

TYPE C

Irregular one-off major international spectator, or competitive, events that generate limited economic activity, and limited or sporadic media coverage. These might include world championships in a 'fringe' media sport (and fashions change) – for example, badminton – or they may include youth, women's or seniors (masters and past masters) championships. Junior championships, such as in boxing or swimming, carry a much higher risk in terms of their ability to attract economic investment. Case studies of economic impacts (see **Chapter 5**) show how volatile this event category is and how difficult it is to forecast the likely economic benefits.

TYPE D

Major competition events or gatherings of enthusiasts that generate limited economic activity with irregular or no media interest, and are usually part of an annual cycle of sport or leisure events. National championships in sports with low spectator appeal usually have limited costs of staging, and their governing bodies have long-term experience in utilising armies of volunteers in putting on and running such events to keep costs low. As the benefits do not outweigh the costs in economic terms, the rationale for bidding for such events is not economic.

Case study: Manchester, urban regeneration and the 2002 Commonwealth Games

On 25 July 2002, Manchester became host to one of the major sporting events in the global sporting calendar, the Commonwealth Games. For the next ten days, over 5000 athletes from 72 competing countries (representing one-third of the world's population) competed for medals in many different events.

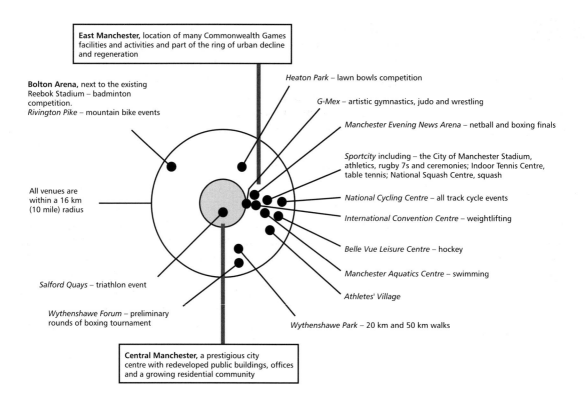

East Manchester, location of many Commonwealth Games facilities and activities and part of the ring of urban decline and regeneration

Bolton Arena, next to the existing Reebok Stadium – badminton competition.
Rivington Pike – mountain bike events

Heaton Park – lawn bowls competition

G-Mex – artistic gymnastics, judo and wrestling

Manchester Evening News Arena – netball and boxing finals

Sportcity including – the City of Manchester Stadium, athletics, rugby 7s and ceremonies; Indoor Tennis Centre, table tennis; National Squash Centre, squash

National Cycling Centre – all track cycle events

International Convention Centre – weightlifting

Belle Vue Leisure Centre – hockey

Manchester Aquatics Centre – swimming

Athletes' Village

All venues are within a 16 km (10 mile) radius

Salford Quays – triathlon event

Wythenshawe Forum – preliminary rounds of boxing tournament

Wythenshawe Park – 20 km and 50 km walks

Central Manchester, a prestigious city centre with redeveloped public buildings, offices and a growing residential community

Figure 2.8 The venues of the Commonwealth Games and the regeneration of East Manchester

It had always been the intention of the City of Manchester Council and other key backers of the Games that the benefits of the competition should be felt in the local community and the city region long after the athletes had gone home and the enormous quantities of banners and hanging baskets had disappeared. Most obviously, those benefits should include the continuing use of the facilities provided at the different venues of the Games (**2.8**). For example, the 38 000-seater Stadium will become home to Manchester City Football Club, starting in the 2003–2004 season; Bolton Arena will now stage Davis Cup tennis matches, and the Squash Centre will be the new home of the Squash Rackets Association. In addition to making world-class sports facilities available for local community use, the targets of the organising committee were to raise Manchester's global image, to create jobs, to encourage investment and, above all, to stimulate the urban regeneration of run-down and deprived East Manchester.

The urban regeneration programme that is now up and running is referred to as NEM (New East Manchester). The NEM area covers 1100 ha. Due to deindustrialisation, 30 per cent of this is currently vacant (that is, mainly derelict); the population has been falling dramatically; much of the housing stock is substandard; environmental conditions are poor; facilities are few and those that exist are of poor quality; and crime is rampant. Aspects of the New East Manchester (NEM) urban regeneration strategy include (**2.9**):

- locating most of the games venues in the NEM area
- encouraging a ripple effect from the redeveloped and prestigious city centre – in particular, capitalising on its present residential property boom

3 What do you think that achieving European City of Culture status might do for Liverpool or Newcastle–Gateshead?

4 How do you rate the chances that the lasting legacy of the Manchester Commonwealth Games will be the regeneration of East Manchester?

- doubling the existing population to 60 000
- building 12 500 new homes and improving 7000 existing ones
- setting up an inward investment agency
- finding new uses for some 40 ha of derelict land.

It is early days yet, but already a new Asda superstore has opened next to the Stadium in Sportcity (**2.8**). This has created 500 new jobs, with 90 per cent of the employees living with a 15-minute journey – that is, coming from East Manchester.

The Games should help to boost **tourism**. Over 1 million people visited Manchester during the event, and a worldwide audience of many millions saw a vibrant, attractive and welcoming city. It is hoped that this will have a long-term impact on visitors and tourists to the Manchester area. Estimates suggest that the city can expect an extra 300 000 visitors (both business and leisure), who will spend £12 million per year. This has been helped by a clever re-imaging of the city, improved access by air, road and rail, and the publicity given to Manchester's cultural and sporting legacy. Not only this, but the Games did much to rekindle the Mancunians' pride in themselves and their city.

SECTION C

The role of investment in the sport and leisure industry

Figure 2.9 A systems diagram of sports funding

Sport and leisure involve two sets of costs – start-up costs and running costs. The stream of spending on sport comes from an increasingly complex web of public and private finance and funding, as shown in **2.9**.

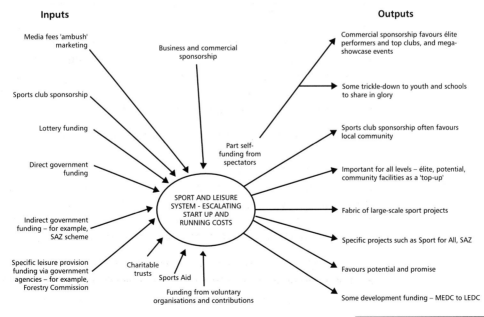

As sport and leisure become more business-orientated, so sources of funding become vital. This is in addition to the money needed for hosting a major event. Sport sponsorship barely existed as an economic activity before 1965, even in the USA. Sponsorship in this context was defined in the Howell Report (1983) as 'the support of a sport, sports event, sport or leisure organisation or competition by an outside body or person for the mutual benefit of both, can be visible (cash) or in kind (equipment and other support)'.

Globally, sport sponsorship today is a massive industry, estimated to be worth around $25 billion (2000), having experienced a growth rate of over 300 per cent during the 1990s. Sport and leisure sponsorship is dominated by large American TNCs, and managed, as is shown in **Chapter 5**, by a number of transnational services organisations.

Sponsorship is very important in ensuring the economic viability of events and teams (**2.10**). It is crucial to the very survival of many. Whilst sponsorship is associated with world events and élite performers, it is also vital for many teams and performers, even at an amateur level. Your school or college team is probably sponsored by free shirts or travel grants by a local sports shop or similar. At a community level, sponsorship can have a very positive impact through involving young people in a variety of sport-based activities, and through coaching courses and educational projects with a strong social emphasis.

Figure 2.10 Sponsorship and the promotion of Manchester United as a global brand (see page 71)

For many large companies, sport sponsorship is their dominant form of sponsorship activity (nearly two-thirds), far more than for the arts. Sport is favoured because of its positive image, feel-good factor and huge media profile. However companies find that there can be diminishing returns from over-long sponsorship. Changing laws – for example, on TV exposure of cigarette sponsorship – are an additional problem, as smoking and alcohol conflict with sport's clean image.

In many countries, some of the proceeds of national lotteries are used to fund sport. In the case of the UK, for every £1 ticket sold, 3.8 pence goes to sport. Between 1996 and 2000 over £1 billion was invested in **capital** projects and a further £100 million in **revenue** schemes to support talented performers.

Whilst there is no doubt that secure funding for athletes can improve performance at major events, and that lottery finance can contribute with other sources of finance to revolutionise the quality of sports provision in countries, many people express concern about the volatility of both sponsorship and lottery funding. The crisis brought about by the collapse of On Digital, and loss of revenue from media rights, has had a disastrous effect on many professional football teams in lower divisions of the English league.

Many would argue that for success in sport and for quality provision in sport and leisure, there is no substitute for direct government funding. The complex web of funding of the sport and leisure system can lead to inequalities at all scales from local to global (**2.9**).

So how does all this link to geography? Well, without the investment there would be a completely different geography of venues, teams, achievement and participation.

Review

5 Look at the sport and leisure system diagram (**2.9**) and undertake the following tasks:

    a Choose three of the funding streams shown and evaluate their strengths and weaknesses.

    b With reference to one chosen large event and one sport, examine the role of sponsorship.

    c To what extent do you think sponsorship should be the major funding source for large-scale events such as the Olympics?

6 Make a list of some of the companies currently sponsoring sporting events. What generalisations can you make about their lines of business?

SECTION D

The value of sport and leisure

Figure **2.11** summarises some of the benefits of the goods and services provided by the sport and leisure industry. For each benefit you can probably turn the statement around to produce a disadvantage (see Review 7 at the end of the chapter). This section will look at some of the less tangible (that is, harder to measure) benefits of sport.

Figure 2.11 The benefits of the sport and leisure industry

Sport and leisure

- Can help to heal international conflicts
- Can provide a service of visual excitement and bring aesthetic benefits
- Success can lead to a great sense of well-being and pride in the nation
- Can provide interest to a variety of landscapes and environments
- Can improve people's quality of life, add to their inclusion in society and promote high standards of health and fitness
- Can provide a major source of income and employment around the world

Quality of life

Over the last 50 years there has been growing evidence of the desirability of regular participation in sport and leisure exercise for physical health reasons, and of having leisure pursuits to maintain a sense of well-being. This has justified increasing government interest in promoting sport and leisure participation by providing finance to ensure access for all to appropriate affordable facilities (for example, Sport for All).

A number of significant epidemiological studies of exercise and sport have found that those who reported vigorous physical exercise had less than half the risk of coronary heart disease. It was subsequently found that physical exercise had a beneficial effect on the prevention of depression, obesity, diabetes and even asthma (see case study in **Chapter 6**, page 79). Public health policies, such as those developed by the Sports Council and Health Education Authorities, are focused on:

■ Providing advice about the benefits of exercise and offering subsidised opportunities (for example, reduced golf and gym subscriptions).
■ Releasing scarce health resources for the use of others, so that they can deal with less easily preventable problems. This could especially benefit the elderly and low-income earners.
■ Increasing productivity, with fewer days lost at work from illness, by offering workplace fitness programmes and lower-cost medical insurance for screening.
■ Identifying the risks and benefits of certain eating habits and offering advice and support on exercise and fitness strategies, as in Sports Action Zones (see the Stoke-on-Trent case studies in **Chapters 3** and **6**, pages 43 and 82).

Set against these benefits there are the negative costs of sports injuries. Research suggests that sports such as rugby, martial arts, hockey, cricket and soccer can cause substantial injuries to regular players. Unsupervised vigorous sport can also lead to long-term health problems such as bone and muscle degeneration.

A further issue associated with well-being and improved quality of life is the claim that participation in sport will improve life for many who would otherwise be attracted to delinquency and vandalism, and begin a life of crime. The provision of sporting and leisure opportunities for young males (the main perpetrators) has been a prime consideration in many inner-city deprived areas with large numbers of socially excluded people. Whilst there is some evidence that crime and vandalism decrease with the loss of the boredom factor, many programmes are only poorly evaluated. For some, the desire to achieve in sport actually leads to the taking of drugs such as anabolic steroids in body-building gyms. A further issue is that spectator sport can be associated with hooliganism and violence, and many people who live near poorly organised venues perceive this as the major negative externality (see **Chapter 4**).

Another way in which sport and leisure can contribute to the quality of life and to a sense of **well-being** is through the provision of natural and artificial products and facilities. Where a country sets aside large areas of lakes (or even reservoirs), mountains, rivers and coastlines and designates them as national parks or other types of conservation area, this helps to ensure public access and enjoyment. It creates a sense of aesthetic enjoyment. Good management promotes quiet enjoyment, yet at the same time conserves those resources for the physical enjoyment of future generations. Only where congestion and over-use occurs do conflicts develop between rural users and the ideals of recreation (fully exposed in **Chapter 4**).

National pride

Success in international sport has long been recognised as being of great value for the whole nation, not only in terms of raising morale, but also in the generation of role models who inspire young people to take part and achieve in sport. Many of the benefits of international sporting success are totally inclusive, as everyone can enjoy success, particularly when heroic performances are involved.

The Coe Report (1985) summarised the public good of sporting excellence as follows:

- Sporting success for Britain makes people proud to be British. Sporting failure or decline has the reverse effect.
- If our teams and individuals are successful (see the medals table in **3.3** on page 29), they help the country's image abroad.
- Sporting achievement in the Olympics and other top competitions is also a vital contribution to the government's and the Sports Council's strategies to boost participation in sport and recreation.
- Sporting achievement has a short-term economic effect – it can sell flags, shirts and various forms of memorabilia.

Australia is frequently cited as a model of sporting achievement and excellence. The following extract from an Australian Institute of Sport teaching pack for Year 6 students, on the role of the Institute, encapsulates the link between sport and national pride:

> *You are part of a great sporting nation. There is something special about the relationship that Australians share with sport. Whether they are participants or spectators, most Australians incorporate sport into everyday lives. The question is why do so many Australians link sport explicitly to our national character? Why do Australians react so strongly to the success of our sporting heroes? Australia is such a diverse nation, and sporting victories provide great opportunities to unite all Australians with patriotic fervour.*

The Australian mass media deliver an image of a healthy 'active' population. People are encouraged to become more like their sporting heroes. Sport is an integral part of Australian culture and the way of life. Since Australians come from a wide variety of global regions and social backgrounds, they achieve across a huge range of sports.

The case study below indicates how important sporting achievement can be to some of the poorest countries in the world.

Case study: What the World Cup did for Senegal – or did it?

Senegal had never qualified for the World Cup before, but in the opening game of the 2002 tournament they beat France, the reigning world champions – a real David and Goliath fairytale. 'Look at France and look at us', wrote the editor of Senegal's oldest newspaper after the match. 'The victory is not just about football, it's about showing the world that when we work hard in Senegal we can succeed in the same way as the people of Europe. A successful football team is the expression of a confident nation, one in which there is democracy and stability and human rights. Psychologically this win (and reaching the quarter finals) is everything for us.'

Remember that more than two-thirds of Senegal's adult population is illiterate and only 1 in 50 owns a TV set. If you arrange the countries of the world in order of wealth, Senegal ranks number 171. It is one of the 50 poorest LEDCs.

As the sports correspondent of another local paper put it: 'a win for Senegal is a win for Africa'. The poverty of Senegal is symbolised by the state of the national stadium (it can hold 60 000 people on hard stone benches raised above a bald brown pitch) and by the filthy ageing minibus used for transporting the national team. It is sights such as these that infuriate the grandfather of Patrick Viera, the greatest footballer that Senegal has ever produced (he plays for France and Arsenal). 'What use', he asks, 'is national confidence and pride, if it evaporates after the World Cup, leaving Senegal in as pitiful an economic state as it was before?'

In conclusion, it has been shown in this chapter that sport and leisure can be a driving force for the good in a range of contexts, particularly the economic and social. Just before the 2002 World Cup, a game of football between North Korea and South Korea also showed that sport can even beat a path towards peace. But as will become evident in **Chapter 4**, there is a down side too.

Review

7 Draw a second diagram to match 2.11 and show the disadvantages of sport and recreation, and how all the benefits can turn into costs.

Enquiry

1 Research examples to support the beneficial value of sport.

2 At the end of this chapter you should be able to research a report on:
   a The factors that influence the demand for, and the supply of, sport and leisure facilities.
   b The importance of sport and leisure in economic development.

Spatial variations in sport and leisure

A key fact in the geography of sport and leisure is that there are significant spatial variations. The types of sport and leisure activity vary from place to place, as do the levels of opportunity and provision. The degree to which a population takes part in sport and leisure is another significant variable, and it is this that provides the focus for the early part of this chapter. The term widely used here is **participation rate**. This simply refers to the proportion of a group of people or whole population engaging in a particular sport and leisure activity.

SECTION A

Participation rates

The concept of participation rates in sport can be explored at a number of different levels, from foundation to élite, as defined in the 'house of sport' (**3.1**).

Figure 3.1 The house of sport

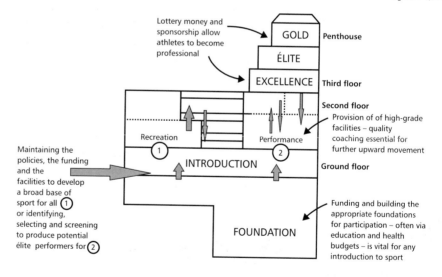

There are a number of different ways of measuring participation. First, questionnaires and surveys of a sample of the population can be used to estimate mass participation in a number of designated sports. Possible indicators derived from such data include:

■ the **index of penetration** – the percentage of people who have ever played a sport

- the **index of fidelity** – the number of adults who still play a particular sport, as a percentage of those who have ever played it
- the **index of intensity** – the ratio between those who claim to play a particular sport and those who can be audited as participating regularly.

Secondly, data about the number of clubs and club members are usually available from international and national sports governing bodies such as the Lawn Tennis Association (LTA). This can give a good idea of the number of competent and active performers in each sport. Bale (2000) has shown how it is then possible to calculate a per capita **index of player production** for a particular town, county or region. This assesses the concentration of a particular sport in relation to national levels. The calculation of this index is shown in the box below. It can be very useful in identifying 'talent hotspots' (see **Section D**).

Index of player production

$$I = \frac{(N/P)}{(1/n)}$$

where I is the per capita index of player production, N is the number of players 'produced' in a given area (for example, a town or a county), P is the population of that area and n is the number of people per player 'produced' in the area as a whole.

For example, if the area had a population of 900 000 and 'produced' 20 players, N/P = 20/900 000, and if there was one player for every 23 000 of the national population, $1/n$ = 1/23 000, the formula would be

$$I = \frac{(20/900\,000)}{(1/23\,000)} = 0.51$$

The national per capita index is always 1.00. An area (county or region) with an index of 2.00 would be 'producing' at twice the national average, and one with an index of 0.5 at half the national average.

Thirdly, the ranking lists that are currently available for many competitive sports, such as swimming and athletics, can give an idea of the numbers, age, sex and location (by club) of players at various 'storeys' in the 'house of sport' (**3.1**).

Fourthly, data are available from major international championships. Since certain standards of performance usually have to be reached before participation is allowed, it is possible to assess the number of élite performers from each participating country (that is, the strength of achievement sport at a national and global level – see **3.2**).

Finally, data from the Olympics can be used to record the number of medal winners (the gold level in the house of sport) for both the Winter and Summer games. The overall distribution of the medals awarded at all the Winter Olympics is shown in **3.3**. Note the concentrated medal success in the small 'alpine' nations, with Norway top of the league. By contrast, there is little evidence of smaller nations shining in the Summer Olympics. Medal success can be related to a number of factors, particularly total population, so as to give a per capita index.

Rank	Country	Number of participants in global top 200	Per capita GNP (US$, 1995)
Cross-country rankings			
1	Kenya	38	370
2	Ethiopia	24	120
3	USA	13	26 980
4	Japan	12	39 640
5	Morocco	10	950
6	France	10	19 480
7	Spain	9	13 580
8	Portugal	7	4 890
9	UK	6	18 700
10	Russia	6	1 500
11	Australia	6	18 720
12	Yugoslavia	6	3 000
13	Ireland	6	14 710
14	Ukraine	5	2 000
15	Romania	5	1 640
Golf rankings			
1	USA	96	26 980
2	UK	27	18 700
3	Japan	16	39 640
4	Australia	16	18 720
5	Sweden	13	23 750
6	South Africa	5	3 160
7	Argentina	4	8 030
8	Spain	3	13 580
9	Ireland	2	14 710
10	Germany	2	27 510
11	Zimbabwe	2	540
12	Canada	1	19 398
13	Fiji	1	2 440
14	India	1	340
15	Philippines	1	1 050

Figure 3.2 Global participation at an élite level in two sports

Country	Number of medals
Norway	236
USSR	217
USA	157
Austria	145
West Germany	145
Finland	134
East Germany	118
Sweden	96
Switzerland	91
Canada	78
Italy	76
France	61
The Netherlands	61
Russia	41
Japan	29
Czech Republic	28
UK	17
South Korea	16
China	14
Hungary	6

Figure 3.3 The all-time distribution of medals awarded at the Winter Olympics (top 20 nations)

Once the necessary raw data are to hand, variations in participation in particular sports and the overall view can then analysed in terms of location, social class, gender and age.

Review

1 Study **3.2**.

- Analyse the geographical distribution of the two top 200 rankings shown.
- To what extent does the state of economic development account for any differences you have identified?
- What further factors might explain the different distributions?
- Is it valid to use élite performance to assess participation rates? Give your reasons.

2 Plot the data in **3.3** on an outline map of the world and write a short analytical account of the distribution.

Explaining spatial variations in sport participation

The patterns resulting from participation research reveal markedly different sport profiles for continents, countries and regions. The Americas have a completely different participation profile – with baseball, American football, basketball, ice hockey and soccer as the top contenders – compared with that of the former British Empire, where sports such as cricket and rugby predominate, along with the ubiquitous soccer. Equally, the global distributions of participation in various sport and leisure activities also show significant variations, both spatially and over time. Soccer (football) has diffused to become a truly global game, with over 200 million people playing at a competitive level. The World Cup is very much a 'global village' event, with 1.2 billion people around the world watching the 2002 championships. However, other sports, such as polo, curling and darts, have much more localised distributions.

There are a number of factors that influence the nature of the sports profile and the amount of participation at various 'storeys' in the 'house of sport'. Many operate at a global scale but also apply to a lesser or greater extent at a national and even a local scale.

Physical factors

Physical factors include climate, relief, altitude and even vegetation. For winter sports, a 'snow season' remains a prerequisite, even though it is possible nowadays to create artificial ski-slopes and snow domes, as well as artificial snow when natural conditions fail. For skiing, snow cover is everything. Important considerations include:

- the earliness of the first snow
- the length of the snow season
- the quality and depth of snow cover
- the reliability of snow cover from year to year
- the size of snowfields.

Although snow formation is essentially climate controlled, the variety of nursery slopes and ski-runs available in an area is conditioned by other factors, such as aspect, relief and altitude.

The physical environment can provide an impetus for the development of particular sports. For example, the close proximity to the sea has certainly promoted a mass interest in sailing and other water sports in countries such as the UK and New Zealand. Equally, plunging breakers provide ideal surfing environments in areas such as Hawaii, California and Cornwall. The hilly terrain and forestry tracks in central Wales have encouraged the country to become the top global venue for mountain-biking.

Physical factors such as altitude can lead to physiological adaptations. For example, the increases in red blood cell concentration, in capillarisation, in myoglobin and in ventilation that result from the lower oxygen pressure at altitude have frequently been cited as the main factor in the concentration of élite performers in cross-country and long-distance running in high-altitude countries such as Kenya and Ethiopia.

Case study: The success of the Kenyan long-distance runner

Kenyan athletes are renowned for their performances, particularly over long distances. Their haul of gold medals at major championships over the last few decades speaks for itself. Many people have argued that the Kenyan success is altitude-related, especially since the vast majority of Kenyan runners came from the Rift Valley and live at over 2000 m above sea level. Others have suggested that particular ethnic groups, such as the Nandi, are genetically endowed. Still others have linked the success to tribal customs. The idea that the tradition of running to school through several miles of bush each day helps youngsters to realise their talents may have some truth in it. Equally, there is no doubting that over the years youngsters have been encouraged by a sequence of role models dating back to Kip Keino, who in the 1960s became the first of Kenya's now many world-famous runners. Some would argue that the history of the success dates back to the days of the British Empire, when athletics training was introduced as part of the curriculum in Kenyan public schools. Subsequently, both the police and army have offered secure employment with excellent training opportunities to quality athletes, thus emphasising the importance of 'nurture, not nature'.

This case study serves to make the crucial point that there are no easy answers to explaining great sporting success. It is vital not to

Review

3 Make a list of sports that you think are particularly affected by physical geography.

overemphasise the control that physical environment might exert on sporting activity and performance. The physical environment may be of some significance, but the complex web of history is probably more important. Equally, a purely biological explanation based on genetics has to be rejected.

Kenyan athletes are now part of a global circuit, with the initial opportunities in the 1980s to gain sports scholarships at US colleges now being superseded by an intensive Kenya-based Sport Aid training programme (see **5.10** on page 76). This is funded by a number of countries, including Germany, the UK and China. Today, Kenyan athletes compete widely on the Grand Prix circuit and earn large sums of money. Currently, the flow of male steeplechasers, cross-country runners and marathon runners has continued to grow but, interestingly, some highly talented women have also begun to emerge, in spite of tribal traditions that do not encourage their involvement.

Human factors

Bearing in mind that most sports take place in arenas, in stadiums and on playing fields, many geographers argue that human factors are more important than physical ones, especially where natural environments are not required. Even the appropriate environments for traditional country pursuits, such as hunting, outdoor shooting or fishing, are now managed and artificially stocked.

At the root of participation rates, no matter at what 'storey' of the 'house of sport' you explore, or at whatever scale, there is the **economic factor** of funding and finance. There is a clear correlation between wealth as measured by per capita GNP and the number of participants at all levels in sport. This is particularly significant in sports that require complex and expensive facilities and equipment. For example, football is far more of a global sport than golf. Golf courses and playing members are heavily concentrated in MEDCs and NICs, although privately developed golf courses have spread throughout the world as part of global golf tourism. Even so, this does not mean that golf is a sport with high global participation rates.

Figure 3.4 Sport England's strategy for producing more élite talent

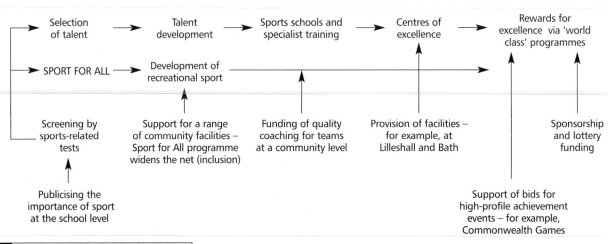

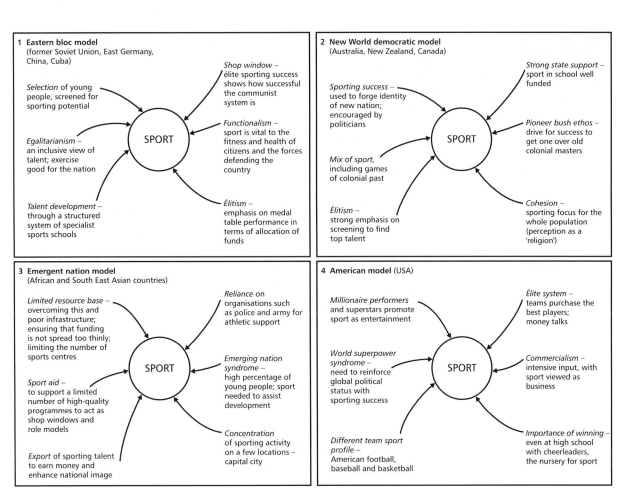

Figure 3.5 Models of four national sports systems

The input of finance and funding by governments is vital in the sports development process. This point is illustrated by the Sport England scheme that was set up in direct response to disappointing performances at the 1992 and 1996 Olympics (**3.4**). This aims to produce élite talent, but recognises the need for a parallel Sport for All policy.

Political factors frequently determine the type of model of adopted by countries in the general organisation of sport. This can have a major impact on participation levels. Whilst the four models in **3.5** share common elements, they differ considerably in terms of their emphases on the élite and the masses, and also in terms of the level of commercialism. Government strategies in MEDCs such as the UK and Spain have also aimed to build facilities in under-resourced areas such as inner cities and rural areas. In the latter, low population densities prevent an economic threshold of operation being reached, so that privately owned facilities lack economic viability.

Geographical factors can lead to 'black holes' in the pattern of sport participation. In many LEDCs that are following the 'emergent model' of sport (**3.5**), limited natural and financial resources mean that certain sports, such as swimming, are under-funded. In the case of élite sports, physical access to quality training is vital. There are certain parts of all countries

4 Of the human factors examined in this section, which do you think has the most powerful influence on participation rates in sport? Give your reasons.

5 Study **3.5** and, for each model:

  ■ explain how political factors have influenced them
  ■ evaluate the effect that the model may have on participation.

6 Draw your own model for sport in the UK. Use the information in **3.5** and research appropriate websites from the list on page 88.

where access to facilities, such as Olympic-size pools, ice rinks and even all-weather facilities, is geographically difficult. This is where boarding education and scholarships for promising talent, as is offered in schools such as Millfield or Kelly College, can make a valuable contribution.

There is no doubt that **historical factors** have a powerful influence on participation rates. The distributions of certain sports, such as rugby and cricket, show how the process of colonisation that created the British Empire also led to the spread of games associated with British public schools. In contrast, baseball has a more concentrated distribution, and is largely linked to the spread of US influence in Central and South America, as well as in Japan. Similarly, the Far East was the core area for martial arts (judo, kick boxing, sumo wrestling and so on), but these sports have now gradually diffused around the world.

Culture can be both a driving force and a constraint in sport participation. Where sporting role models exist, they inevitably have a halo effect on the popularity of particular sports. On the other hand, the constraints of culture are well documented. Issues of gender and ethnicity can limit the number of participants in particular sports, as for example in women's athletics and swimming. Here, the conventional minimal approach to sports clothing can limit the number of Muslim women participants, with world-class performers such as distance athletes from Morocco and Algeria facing considerable disapproval at home. Equally, it is important to disentangle the cultural factors from the economic factors that traditionally limit the participation of women in sport.

Perceptions can be a serious limitation. In the UK, for example, sport is frequently perceived as a non-serious recreation. Some people argue that the enormous success of fun runs actually constricts the supply of serious participants. Many are put off by the need to stick to often tough training regimes. Parents argue that commitment to sport can detract from study. Hopefully the Paula Radcliffe role model will do much to negate this, as will the availability of university sports scholarships at places such as the universities of Bath and Loughborough, for those of world-class potential.

Personal experience may also act as a constraint. Often the first experience of sport is closely linked to education at school. Some argue that poor-quality PE has put many British teenagers off sport, especially girls, whereas in contrast countries such as Australia have developed an extremely pro-sport culture in schools.

Socio-economic factors can also be limiting. There are some 125 000 sports clubs with 6 million members in the UK alone, but the costs of joining many of them are beyond the means of many working-class people. In the case of golf, the costs of club membership, equipment and green fees can be as high as £4000 per year. Even in football – one of the most inclusive of sports, with over 1 million people playing in Sunday leagues – peer group and commercial pressures help to raise the annual cost of active participation to nearly £3000. Thus there are socio-economic constraints based on income differentials. Similarly, there are constraints rooted in social history. Traditional inner-city culture has seen such areas function as nurseries for generations of boxers. Boxing is regarded as a 'working-class' sport, in contrast to polo, for example, which is still seen as exclusively for the upper classes. There is no doubting that factors of this kind persist and so perpetuate class divides in sport.

Explaining spatial variations in leisure participation

Participation rates in leisure, as opposed to organised sport, are closely linked at all scales to per capita GNP. At the global scale, a North–South divide is evident. Because of higher levels of personal wealth, the inhabitants of MEDCs are better placed than those of LEDCs to participate in and enjoy leisure pursuits. In this age of the post-industrial society, MEDC workers also have more time and opportunity to participate. It is the prevailing cultural philosophy today that 'having healthy hobbies is good for body and soul'. So physical recreation is very much up front. However, when it comes to choosing the precise form of recreation, class once again seems to rear its head. Hunting and shooting are perceived as largely upper-class pursuits, whereas activities such as rambling, cycling, bird-watching and fishing tend to be more open across classes, with the last two having a marked gender bias.

The availability of appropriate locations, such as mountains and lakes that can be reached by car for weekend use (as in the English Lake District), is another key factor affecting participation. Activities such as windsurfing, surfing and mountain-biking have become very popular and are now a peripheral part of the fashion culture. Their expansion has been linked to greater availability of transport. Rising car ownership has opened up many remote rural regions. Technological developments in the manufacturing of sports equipment have allowed the mass production of affordable equipment, such as new-style surfboards and multi-geared mountain bikes. Such products have undoubtedly meant more fun for novices and experts alike.

A number of influences associated with business development have also increased participation rates. Leisure has been **commodified** (packaged as a product) by the large-scale involvement of transnational companies (TNCs) in the provision of health and fitness clubs, indoor tennis courts and golf courses (see **Chapter 5 Section E**). This involvement of over 30 such companies in the UK has led to escalating numbers of clubs (over 800) and associated membership (approaching 200 000), so contributing to the health and fitness boom.

Case study: Fitness clubs in fitting locations?

The fitness club is a relative newcomer to the urban sport and leisure scene (**3.6**). Today, the gym business is a big one – in the UK alone it turns over £1.5 billion a year. During the 1990s, the value of the UK fitness business grew by over 80 per cent. In 2001 alone, 156 new health clubs were opened. More than 3 million Britons are now members of a gym.

Figure 3.6 Steps to better fitness

The rise of this leisure business seems to be the outcome of three developments in modern society:

- today's increasingly sedentary lifestyles
- a tendency to overindulge in food and drink, or to consume the wrong substances
- a growing concern about personal looks, health and fitness.

Two major chains of health club dominate the UK business: Fitness First and David Lloyd Leisure. Clubs tend to be set up in three type locations:

- within affluent suburbs
- close to the employment nodes of central urban areas
- on main arterial roads between workplaces and homes.

Overall, location and convenience are critical. As one chain manager has put it, '... people are inherently lazy. They drive up to our clubs and try to get the parking spot nearest the entrance.' This raises the issue of whether the lack of a car might create a degree of exclusion.

By advertising and programme scheduling, media companies play a major role in influencing and supporting fashion trends in leisure clothing and equipment. The marketing of leisure is now very sophisticated and increasingly manipulates consumer behaviour. The basic aim is to create an enormous desire for a 'hot' product: in 2002, all types of neoprene and Lycra® surf-wear became part of high fashion.

Consumerism emphasises the value of consumption, change and innovation: hence the almost constant widening of the range of leisure pursuits, helped along by new technology. The current extreme ('X') sports boom is one such example. Politics can also be very influential, as governments attempt to re-create or create an overall 'spirit of the times' by:

- supporting legislation (for example, to ban fox hunting or to promote gambling)
- shifting the burden of taxation to create more disposable income
- introducing social inclusion strategies that emphasise the importance of a wide range of leisure activities.
- defining policy frameworks for leisure.

The indirect impact of government actions is frequently underestimated. For example, government grants for farm diversification have fuelled a boom in pheasant shooting, with 36 million pheasants being reared for one of the UK's fastest growing leisure activities. This now takes place on over 2000 estates or farms. The industry is estimated to have an annual turnover of £600 million and to employ over 25 000 people.

Case study: Surfing in the UK – a new national obsession

Surfing has recently experienced an unprecedented surge in popularity. The British Surfing Association (BSA) estimates that over 250 000 people are surfing regularly. Between 200 and 2002 membership almost tripled, with more than 50 000 people being introduced to the sport each year. Part of the credit must go to the effective packaging of surf culture. In 2002, £160 million was spent on surf-branded merchandise. Today there is a surf-wear shop in most shopping malls, even in landlocked areas. The profits have helped to bankroll competitions, such as that held at Newquay (Cornwall), the only leg of the World Professional Tour to take place in the UK.

Helping to increase participation rates are those technological advances that have made the sport more user-friendly. These include wet suits crafted in neoprene, and longer, wider surfboards which, because of their new materials, are much easier to use and manoeuvre. This surfboard revolution has brought back retired surfers. The sport has also become more 'woman-friendly', with women being the faster-growing market. Finally, cheap, low-cost flights from London (Stansted) to Newquay have made a surfing weekend in Cornwall more feasible for many enthusiasts.

One remaining problem at Britain's top surfing spots, Newquay and Bournemouth, is that erratic sea conditions mean that 'big curl' type waves only form spasmodically. It might be possible to rectify this by constructing artificial reefs that permanently generate big waves. This would give British surfers the chance to practice in good conditions all year round. Then there is the weather: rain and cool temperatures mean that the British venues do not compare with Hawaii, Bondi Beach or Los Angeles.

There is a huge spin-off (multiplier effect) from the surfing industry (hotels, accommodation, food, equipment and rentals, and so on). This is very important for Cornwall, a county of high unemployment with EU Category 1 status for support. So everybody wants to keep the participation rates up, and wants Newquay to retain its top ranking as a UK surfing venue.

This case study indicates that, as in organised sport, leisure participation rates are the result of both physical and human factors. One major difference is that the latter are more difficult to measure, as participation in activities such as bird-watching, rambling and climbing is often very informal. Therefore questionnaires and surveys provide the main source of data, inevitably from a sample population. But there are exceptions. Take orienteering, for example (see case study below). This is considered to be a sport by some and a leisure pursuit by many.

Case study: Orienteering in the USA

Orienteering clubs are located in 38 states, with concentrations in the Pacific Northwest and the Atlantic Northeast. Whilst certain physical conditions – such as hilly terrain and wooded areas, as opposed to open countryside or mountains – are required, these alone do not explain the distribution (3.7). Most clubs are located in the rural–urban fringe and where there is ready access from the more affluent middle-class suburbs.

Figure 3.7 The distribution of orienteering clubs in the USA

Researchers consider the demographics of the local area to be the most important factor; namely, a population in which the 25–40 age range is well represented, and there is a high incidence of graduates and high-earning professionals. The spatial diffusion of the sport over time has also been found to be a key factor. The original home of US orienteering was the Delaware valley in the Northeast, but club leaders subsequently happened to migrate (often for employment reasons) to Missouri and to the Northwest, and they established clubs in these new locations. A further factor initially considered important was proximity to large military bases. This was based on the observation that service personnel frequently participate in orienteering competitions. However, statistical analysis has found the link to be weak.

As with other participation studies, care has to be taken not to jump to deterministic conclusions about influencing factors. It is the interplay of physical and human geography that explains the distribution.

Review

7 Explain the possible link between the four causal factors mentioned in the case study and the distribution shown in 3.7.

The creation of sport and leisure hotspots

The term **hotspot** is used to describe an area in which there is an above average or greater than expected concentration of sport or leisure activity. This is another manifestation of spatial variation. Such concentrations often have environmental and economic consequences – hence the use of a term that is indicative of overheating.

There are many different types of hotspot. Examples of single-activity hotspots would include trekking in Nepal and sex tourism in Thailand. Examples of multiple-activity hotspots are provided by Manchester for sport (see page 19) and by Sun City (South Africa), Santa Monica (see case study below) and Las Vegas for leisure activities. Investors in sport and leisure hotspots prefer multiple activities, as they decrease the risks associated with changing tastes. Such hotspots are also more likely to enjoy year-round, non-seasonal usage and therefore maximum economic benefits.

Case study: The Santa Monica leisure hotspot

A study of Santa Monica shows how a number of chance factors, such as nearness to Hollywood, combine with certain physical and human advantages to create a unique fitness hotspot for urban athletes.

Santa Monica, a westerly beach suburb of Los Angeles, is located next to a superb 5 km golden beach on the Pacific Ocean, with a pleasant Mediterranean climate suitable for outdoor action (there are over 330 days of sunshine per year). It became a fitness resort with the opening of Muscle Beach (an alfresco gym) in the 1930s. The enterprise of local businesses was a further contributory factor. Today, Santa Monicans power walk, do t'ai chi, surf, cycle, run, kick box, get harmonic massages and eat only in restaurants that conform to the rigorous dietary requirements of the latest diet fads.

The facilities for outdoor action, such as a 40 km bike trail and outstanding surfing, are combined with a range of artificial developments such as The Cage – an outdoor gym favoured by stars such as Arnold Schwarzenegger – and outstanding athletics field and track facilities. A cluster of gyms provides a wide range of fitness classes combined with the necessary facilities for chilling out and beautification, all of the highest quality and using the latest technology.

This agglomeration means that Santa Monica is well placed to develop a tourist strand to its essentially local leisure industry, which is currently estimated to employ around 2000 people.

Hotspots occur at a range of scales from local to international. A typology of hotspots might distinguish between those that develop *in situ* at particular locations and those that result from migration. Equally, a distinction might be made between natural hotspots – such as the Himalayas for trekking and mountaineering – and those, such as Santa Monica and Las Vegas, that are artificially generated.

A hotspot may exhibit some or all of the following features (**3.8**):

- A concentration of facilities for one or more sport and/or leisure facilities. The Las Vegas Strip is a prime example. Inevitably, as in the case of Pat Pong Street (the sex street of Bangkok), such concentrations enjoy the advantages of agglomeration economies. Hotspots may also be specifically designed to generate a multiplier effect, as happened in Manchester during the Commonwealth Games (see page 19).
- An above-average participation rate in key sporting or leisure activities. This may be temporary, as with the staging of a major world event, or designed to generate year-round income with maximum use of facilities (as in the Sun City mega-resort in South Africa).
- A concentration of employment in particular sporting or leisure-related activities, as measured by the location quotient. For example, the Sportcity development in Manchester was designed to provide a wide range of sport- and leisure-related employment.
- A concentration of achievement and élite talent, such as star footballers or basketball players. South-east Brazil could be regarded as a talent hotspot for footballers – as could Rio de Janeiro, for the beach volleyball players who train on Copacabana (see also **5.9** on

Figure 3.8 Types of sporting hotspot

There are many types of sporting hotspot, at local, regional and global scales. These can be broken down into two main categories: **locational** and **talent** hotspots.

Locational hotspots are found all over the globe. These are the massive stadiums, the Olympic cities and the World Cup host nations. Some – such as Wimbledon – will be active every year, whereas others appear in the spotlight only for a short time, but remain a centre for sport.

As the term suggests, **talent hotspots** are centres of talent. Brazil is a football talent hotspot, producing many of the world's finest players (the likes of Ronaldo and, historically, Pele). Despite this, it is not a locational hotspot – the best Brazilians enter the Western European leagues of Spain, Italy, England and Germany.

Locational hotspots do not necessarily generate local talent. No British man has won Wimbledon for 90 years. Neither Japan nor South Korea produce a huge number of world-class footballers, and recent winners of the Tour de France have not been French.

Similarly, Spain produces some of the finest tennis players and golfers, Arantxa Sanchez Vicario and Sergio Garcia amongst them, yet in neither sport does the country host a major global tournament, with the possible exception that Valderama will host the next Ryder Cup.

However, these are not two mutually exclusive categories. Some places excel in both (for example, US Open tennis: Agassi and Sampras), while others suffer a dearth of either category (for example, Egypt: world-class downhill skiers).

Perhaps there is a connection between location and talent for the development and sustainability of hotspots. One may possibly lead to the other.

page 74). Centres of excellence are another form of talent hotspot, and emerge as a consequence of superb facilities, quality coaching and scholarships to help meet the costs of attendance.

An interesting exercise is to ask people where they perceive the hotspots of particular sports to be (**3.9**).

Figure 3.9 The perception of sporting hotspots in the UK, 1998

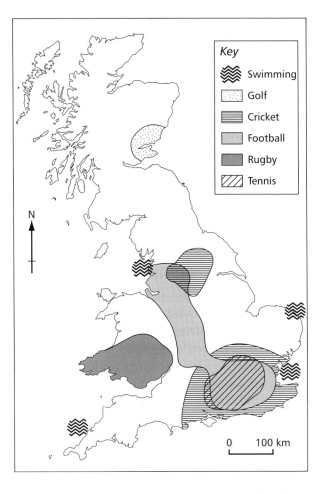

Key
- Swimming
- Golf
- Cricket
- Football
- Rugby
- Tennis

N

0   100 km

Why do hotspots develop?

A number of physical, sociocultural and economic factors combine to create a **locational hotspot** (**3.8**). Scotland, for example, is a golf hotspot. A vital factor here is the fact that golf was actually invented in Scotland, nearly 800 years ago. It started as a game to be played on sea-washed turf, dry sand dunes and naturally undulating ground – the prime ingredients of today's challenging links course. Turnberry and St Andrews are ranked amongst the top 20 golf courses in the world. Good accessibility and an up-market image, much appreciated by Americans, have ensured Scotland's continuing reputation as the home of global golf.

Sociocultural factors of a similar historical kind have made the MCC at Lords and the All England Tennis Club at Wimbledon in London the spiritual hotspots of cricket and tennis respectively. The case studies of Sheffield (page 17) and Manchester (page 19) have shown that economic factors can play their part in the creation of hotspots, particularly when there is government backing.

As for talent hotspots, wealth is of great importance, as those with 'means' have the best access to top-class facilities, training grounds, equipment and quality coaching. Talent hotspots can also develop as a result of migration induced by transfer deals, as to Premier League clubs in England. In LEDCs, there are fewer facilities to exploit sports potential. It is for this reason that talented young players so often migrate to MEDCs. Some countries, such as Brazil, seem to be 'natural' reservoirs of sporting talent, whilst other talent hotspots have developed through political influences. A number of former communist regimes, such as those of East Germany and Romania, saw achievement sport success as reflecting favourably on the nation (**3.5**). Extreme coaching methods and even drug supplements were used to achieve top performance levels in athletics, gymnastics and football. As seen in the case study of Kenyan runners (page 31), a combination of physical and human factors can produce an environment in which a talent hotspot develops.

Review

8 Suggest possible ways of measuring the relative status of different locational or talent hotspots.

Sport and leisure in the city

In a loose and general sense, cities might be perceived as locational hotspots, if only by virtue of their dense concentrations of population, which support dense networks of sport and leisure opportunities. Figure **3.10** attempts to model the development of that network in the UK.

Figure 3.10 A model of the main phases in the growth of UK urban sport and leisure

As one moves away from the city centre, significant changes in sport and leisure may be detected, as well as recurring spatial patterns that pivot around the CBD (**3.11**). The changes are the outcome of (i) the six interacting factors considered in **Chapter 2 Section A** and (ii) five different planning influences:

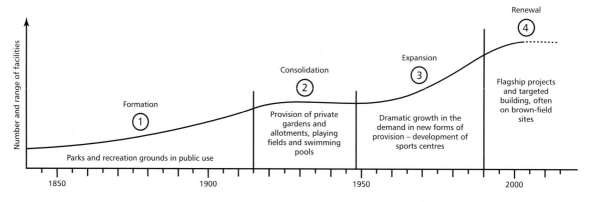

Figure 3.11 A model of sport and leisure development in and beyond the MEDC city

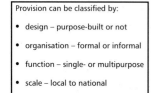

Provision can be classified by:
- design – purpose-built or not
- organisation – formal or informal
- function – single- or multipurpose
- scale – local to national
- source – public or voluntary

- the **standards approach** – sports facilities such as playing fields are provided on the basis of a per capita national standard
- the **spatial approach** – to ensure equity of provision across the built-up area
- the **organic approach** – this allows sports centres to develop in the places where they are likely to be successful
- the **hierarchical approach** – this involves a Christaller-like ordering of facilities across the built-up area, with flagship developments having city-wide catchments
- the **community development approach** – whereby deprived communities are awarded quality facilities via bids.

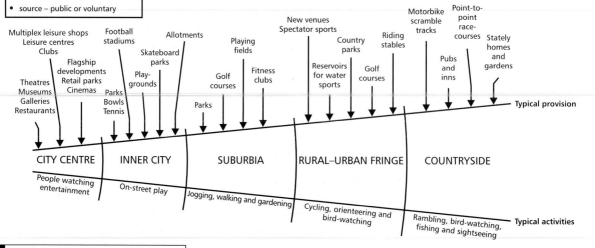

The case study of Stoke-on-Trent below illustrates how all these approaches have contributed to the distribution of key facilities within the built-up area.

Case study: The distribution of three sports facilities in Stoke-on-Trent

Stoke has a somewhat complicated structure, which reflects the fact that it is a small conurbation made up of six, once separate, Potteries towns.

The distribution of **fitness centres**, many of which are private enterprises, shows elements of the **organic approach (3.12)**. Key locational factors would seem to be ease of access and proximity to the original town centres (see earlier case study on page 36). There is some evidence of a **spatial approach**, but note the areas of deficit in the north-east of the built-up area. Abbey Hulton is a deprived area of social welfare housing. Here, only a community development approach using public funds holds out any hope of rectifying the deficiency. Some elements of a **hierarchy** might be detected within the fitness business, with the Fenton Manor centre seen as a city-wide, top-level facility.

Swimming pool provision bears some resemblance to a **standards approach**, with pools dispersed around the city, but this is largely a result of the way in which the conurbation developed, with each of the six towns originally having municipal facilities in the form of a pool and a public park. The important role of the new high-school sports centres, such as Holden Lane and Sandon, for community use will do much to plug the gaps.

Golf courses have a peripheral distribution, as expected in the model (see **3.11**), with much of the provision in the more affluent south and west of the city. Parkhall and Golden Hill are community provided and do much to improve standards of provision spatially across the city.

It is hoped that this chapter has served to illustrate one of the basic truths of geography, namely that no two places are alike. In the context of sport and leisure, there are considerable spatial variations, at different spatial scales, in both opportunities and participation. These two facets are, of course, closely interrelated, and together they create a vital dimension in the geography of sport and leisure. One obvious outcome is the creation of hotspots and, in their wake, areas that fare less well.

Review

9 Select a large urban area of your choice.

- Map and analyse the distribution of a range of indoor and outdoor sport and leisure facilities.
- Compare your results with the model **3.11**.

Figure 3.12 The distribution of three kinds of sports facility in Stoke-on-Trent

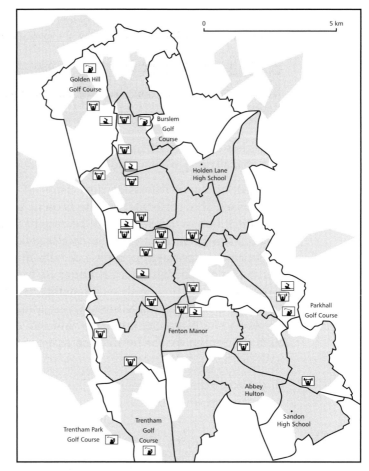

Key

[icon] Health and fitness clubs

[icon] Golf courses

[icon] Swimming pools

Labels on map:
Golden Hill Golf Course
Burslem Golf Course
Holden Lane High School
Parkhall Golf Course
Fenton Manor
Abbey Hulton
Sandon High School
Trentham Park Golf Course
Trentham Golf Course

Review

10 Make a copy of people's perceptions of hotspots for six sports in the UK, as shown for 1988 in **3.9**.

- Ask ten people to explain why they think these places have been selected as hotspots.
- Carry out the exercise again, this time asking ten people (across a range of age groups) to identify, on a blank map, where they think the hotspots are for rugby, golf, cricket, football, tennis and swimming. Are there are any changes compared with 1988?

Enquiry

You should now be able to research the topic 'Sport and Uneven Development' (see **Further reading and resources** on page 87). Two key questions to research are:

- What factors influence the levels and nature of participation in sport and leisure activities?
- What factors (physical, economic, social, environmental, technological and political) lead to the development of sport and leisure hotspots?

The impacts of sport and leisure

When it comes to considering the impacts of sport and leisure, it is tempting to think only in positive terms. After all, at a personal level, sport and leisure are meant to be therapeutic. They are to be enjoyed and the expectation is that they will enhance our health and quality of life. **Chapter 2 Section B** and **Chapter 5** draw our attention to the economic multipliers and benefits associated with the staging of major sporting events. However, in reality, sport and leisure are no exception to the general rule that human activities generate both costs and benefits. There are negative effects that directly impact on people, such as injury or increased admission charges to a leisure facility. There are also indirect negative effects, because sport and leisure can and do have adverse effects on places and environments. Examples are hooliganism among sports supporters and Bank Holiday traffic congestion. In other words, they are the sorts of thing that spoil enjoyment. In this chapter, attention will focus on impacts that might be broadly classified as environmental.

SECTION A

Externalities

Figure 4.1
The spillover effects of a sports facility

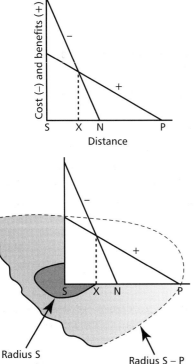

Radius S

Radius S – P

When discussing the impact of major sporting events and facilities, reference is often made to externalities, positive and negative, rather than costs and benefits. **Externalities** are the spillover effects that ripple out from a source. Perhaps the best example is the football stadium. Its negative effects are those that impose the costs of staging a football match not on the players or spectators, but on local residents. For example, traffic congestion around the stadium on match days prevents local people from parking close to their homes or from even using their cars. Noise, litter and vandalism are other costs that spring to mind. At the same time, positive externalities might include the increased business on match days enjoyed by a pub or 'chippy' that happens to be located near the football ground. Most externalities show a distance-decay characteristic. The positive and negative effects decline with increasing distance from, in this case, the football stadium and so create **externality gradients (4.1)**. In **4.1** the negative effects decline more rapidly than the positive. Between the stadium (S) and X, the negative effects are supreme, but beyond those effects are outweighed by the positive. Indeed, beyond N there are no negative spillover effects.

The concept of externalities also applies to many forms of leisure. Just think of the spillover effects of some of the outside-the-home activities shown in **1.2** (see page 5), such as pubs and clubs, cinemas and theatres. A geographical approach to the impacts of both sport and leisure activities involves exploring four aspects of the spillover effect:

- the kinds of impact that specific activities have on communities and environments
- the spatial range over which those particular impacts are experienced
- the actual gradients – that is, the degree to which they decay with distance
- the overall balance of positive and negative impacts, and how that balance changes with distance.

In the next section, attention is focused on the externalities of sport, and in particular on those of sports arenas and major events. It so happens that most of these are located or take place in towns and cities. But those same towns and cities are also home to a great diversity of everyday sport and leisure. This is simply because most of us live in an urban environment. It is also because participation in sport and leisure is something that we weave into our schedules outside the working day. Participating during lunch breaks and evenings means that we must play mainly near to home or work. This will be explored in **Section C**. On occasions, however, particularly at weekends, we do escape the urban area. When we do, as will be illustrated in **Section D** and **Section E**, so our sport and leisure begin to impact on the countryside and on water environments, be they rivers, lakes or the sea.

Review

1 Explain and illustrate what is meant by an **externality**.

2 Why do negative externalities decay with distance?

3 Draw a table that sets out the externalities of a Grand Prix motor-racing circuit such as Silverstone.

SECTION B

The externalities of stadiums and events

Some of the basic externalities of established sports arenas, such as stadiums, have already been outlined, so the discussion now moves on to consider the spillover effects of three particular situations:

- the expansion of an existing stadium
- the relocation of a sports stadium or ground
- the staging of a major sporting or leisure event.

The first two scenarios will be illustrated by references to football grounds, and the third by looking at a leisure event that is popular with the young – the pop festival.

Scenario 1

The tragedy at Hillsborough football ground in April 1989 and the public inquiry that followed drew public attention to the fact that many football stadiums in the UK were dangerous. The Taylor Commission set out two courses of action to remedy the situation. One option was for all Football

League stadiums to be converted into lower-density, all-seater facilities. Most clubs chose this option. A small number, however, opted for the more radical option of building anew, often on a site away from the existing stadium.

In both cases, there have been negative externalities in the form of local opposition. In the first scenario, upgrading an existing stadium, there have been strong expansion pressures. To accommodate the same number of spectators seated as opposed to standing has required more space and the raising of the height of grandstands, as even prestige clubs such as Liverpool and Manchester United have found to their cost. On top of this, since league football is now a multimillion-pound business, it is imperative that stadium capacities are increased and made more comfortable. The problem has been that this expansion of existing stadiums has not taken place without adversely affecting people living nearby. It has not just been a matter of scaling up the negative externalities of the old stadium. There have been additional costs, particularly in the short term. These have included the compulsory acquisition and demolition of dwellings – often requiring the rehousing of poorer families – and the noise, dust and general disruption caused by construction work. In the long term, there are negative externalities such visual disamenity and the blocking out of sunlight.

Scenario 2

Those football clubs that have decided to relocate have faced two rather different problems. The first has been to overcome the widespread perception that a football stadium is a 'noxious facility' that nobody wants near their home. Residents living near prospective relocation sites have proved to be highly vocal in their opposition. A study of the relocated stadium of St Johnstone Football Club in Perth showed that its negative externality field was greater in spatial extent than that of its old city-centre ground.

Local groups have proved themselves capable of mounting well-organised campaigns to resist the relocation of stadiums, forcing public inquiries and performing persuasively at meetings. Surprisingly, perhaps, relocation has proved unpopular with fans. Traditionally, they have developed a special sentimental attachment to their 'home' ground, and for this reason there has been a considerable resistance to any change. You can readily imagine that Wimbledon FC's recent proposal to move to Milton Keynes did not go down well with their London supporters! But in making this seemingly outlandish proposal, it is possible that the club was pursuing another agenda. Not only was it intent on finding a relatively cheap site for a new stadium, but it also was hoping to tap into the supporter potential of a large and very prosperous city that currently lacks a top-flight professional football team.

At present, the relocation of stadiums to green-field sites in or just beyond the suburbs is not popular with planners. Their preference is that inner-city, brown-field sites should be used. It has to be said that there have been successful ventures; that is, in terms of reviving run-down areas and reducing the general level of negative externalities. A recent example is provided by the shift of Southampton FC to a site even closer to the city centre than its old ground.

Case study: The Saints go marching in, but cricket moves out ...

When Southampton FC (the 'Saints', as they are popularly known) moved into the Dell in 1898, the stadium was located on the edge of the city and was one of the most modern stadiums in the country. By the time they moved out in May 2001, it was woefully inadequate for the needs of a Premiership club. Following the Taylor Report, the need to go all-seater had cut the ground's capacity to a mere 15 200. With finances increasingly ruling the game, and with local opposition to any *in situ* enlargement, it became clear that the only way for the club to survive was to move to a new and larger stadium. The idea finally got off the ground in 1996, when the club gained the Stock Market listing that it needed to raise much of the necessary capital.

The first choice site for a new stadium was a 60-acre (24.25 ha) plot on the outskirts of the city at Stoneham. It looked ideal. It was right by the M27, Southampton Airport and Southampton Parkway Station. With the provision of ample car parking space as an integral part of the plans, the whole issue of transport and access seemed well sorted. But the site in question was located on the boundary between two planning authorities – the Labour-held City Council and the Liberal Democrat Eastleigh Borough Council. The Tory-controlled Hampshire County Council owned the actual site.

Figure 4.2 St Mary's – the new home of the Saints in central Southampton

Given this complex 'political location', it was hardly surprising that the three authorities were unable to agree to the stadium development. However, the City Council quickly came up with an alternative site, albeit one without such good transport links. It was near to the city centre, on the site of a former gas works (**4.2**). Planning permission was rushed through, archaeological concerns about the site were satisfied and funds were raised through a £17 million loan. Clearance of the site began in August 1999 and the first game was played exactly two years later at the 32 500-seat, state-of-the art stadium. It is more than fitting that the new home of the Saints should be in the St Mary's district of Southampton. Happily, the level of negative externalities is now much lower than at the Dell. Official recognition of the quality of the new stadium came in November 2002, when it was the venue for an international match between England and Macedonia.

There is an interesting twist to this relocation story. Virtually at the same time, and like Southampton FC, Hampshire County Cricket Club decided

Figure 4.3 The Hampshire Rose Bowl – a newcomer to Southampton's green belt

to sell its ground in Southampton (located close to the Dell) for residential development and use the proceeds to build a new one elsewhere. It too sought to obtain planning permission for a new site in the green belt, immediately outside the city. As with the Saints, the aim was to take advantage of the good motorway and rail links. It was perhaps surprising that in 1996 the club was given the go-ahead by the three planning authorities to develop a 150-acre (60.75 ha) site at West End. In the same year, it was promised £7 million from the National Lottery fund. Work started in 1997 and the new ground, now called the Hampshire Rose Bowl, was opened in 2001 (**4.3**). The ground has a capacity for 10 000 spectators and offers parking for over 3000 cars. The centrepiece of the development is the main pavilion – a stunning building that is also available throughout the year for hire as a conference centre and for receptions. It also accommodates indoor nets, a multi-gym, squash and aerobic facilities. Other components of the whole project include a sports injuries clinic, a sports shop and a 'pay-as-you-play' golf course.

This study of the relocation of two of Southampton's sports venues raises a number of questions:

- Was there some sort of discrimination against football, its supporters and their stereotypical behaviour?
- Was it believed that the negative externalities of a cricket ground are likely to be less than those of a football stadium?
- Was a cricket ground deemed to be more in keeping with the ethos of the green belt than a football stadium?

It certainly looks as if these two sports did not receive even-handed treatment from the decision-makers.

Scenario 3

The economic benefits of major sporting events are illustrated in **Chapter 2** and again in **Chapter 5**. Since these events involve the construction of new sports arenas and facilities, the same sorts of externality apply as have just been identified. However, there are major events of a less formal nature that, whilst making fewer infrastructural demands, are capable of generating considerable negative externalities. Obvious examples are the so-called 'festivals' (such as those held at Glastonbury, Leeds and Reading) and 'raves'. Often staged in rural settings, such events appeal to the young, but are distinctly unpopular with local residents.

Case study: The externalities of the Glastonbury Festival

The Glastonbury Festival is described as a 'festival of performing arts' and includes almost everything from rock and pop music to juggling, stand-up comedy and crafts. First held in 1970, it now takes place annually over a three-day period in June, on 800 acres (324 ha) of fields located between Glastonbury and the town of Shepton Mallet in Somerset. Annual attendance has risen from 1500 people in 1970 to well over 100 000. But the event is not popular with everyone, particularly local residents.

Opposition to the festival focuses on a number of negative externalities that ripple out from the site. These include:

- **noise** – although there are restrictions on noise levels, local residents have to suffer three days and nights when the level of amplified music reaches 60 decibels
- **crime** – in 2002 there were over 1000 reported crimes attributed to the festival, such as burglary, vandalism, assault and drugs offences
- **traffic congestion** – particularly on country roads around the site
- **air pollution** – traffic congestion is a major source, but smog caused by the burning of plastic on camp-fires is another
- **water pollution** – caused by sewage, oil seepage and soil compaction
- **litter** – great quantities are produced; there is effective on-site collection, but inevitably litter drifts into adjacent areas
- **visual pollution** of a beautiful area of countryside – caused by the many cars, people and tents, as well as the festival's infrastructure of ten open-air stages and other facilities
- **cultural impact** – it is claimed that the 'alternative' culture associated with the festival has adversely affected the shops in Glastonbury.

Supporters of the festival are quick to point out a number of positive externalities. These include:

- **raised levels of local business** – the influx of festival-goers is good news for shops, pubs, cafés and restaurants, and other beneficiaries include local contractors providing on-site services; this externality is claimed to extend to a radius of 20 miles
- **jobs** – a large number of jobs are created just before and after the festival, as well as during it; there is also a small full-time workforce.
- **donations made to local groups** – for example, to some 25 community clubs.

At the time of writing (January 2003), the fate of the festival lies in the balance. Towards the end of 2002, the local authority voted against granting the organisers a public entertainment licence for up to 150 000 people. This effectively means there will be no festival in 2003 – that is, unless the organisers mount a successful appeal against the decision.

Review

4 Discuss the relative merits of green- and brown-field sites as locations for major sports arenas.

5 Compare the negative externalities of football and cricket grounds. Are there significant differences?

6 'Leisure pleasure for tens of thousands or peace and quiet for a few hundred local residents?' Where do your sympathies lie in the Glastonbury stand-off? Give your reasons.

Impacts on the urban environment

In this section we focus not on prestige sporting facilities and events but, rather, on the more routine and basic activities that are an essential part of everyday life for so many urban people. The ten most popular sports in the UK, in order of preference, are walking, swimming, keep fit, snooker, cycling, weight-training, football, golf, running and ten-pin bowling. Although all of these can be, and are, pursued in an urban environment, they vary in terms of their typical locations (see **3.11** on page 42). But what sorts of impact do these sports and popular leisure activities, together with their infrastructures, have on communities and particular parts of the urban environment? What are the impacts of amenities such as leisure centres, sports grounds, clubs (sport and social), swimming pools, fitness centres, pubs, restaurants and cafés, theatres and cinemas, galleries, parks, lakes and ponds? Does the scale of their impact compare with the externalities considered in the two previous sections? The short answer is that they do make an impact, but in general it is less overt (**4.4**). Just pause for a moment to consider the possible externalities of fitness clubs (see the case study in **Chapter 3** on page 36). As with most sport and leisure activities, they are both positive and negative. On the plus side, they often make use of refurbished redundant buildings. They frequently attract linked activities, such as sports shops and, ironically, fast-food outlets (thanks to appetites whetted by exercise!). Traffic and noise are two obvious minuses.

Figure 4.4 Some impacts of sport and leisure on the urban environment

1 **The physical environment**

- land, which may have been used for other purposes, lost to sport and leisure developments
- changes to urban hydrology
- manicuring of water bodies – rivers, ponds and lakes
- modification of topography
- conversion of spoil heaps into dry ski slopes

2 **Visual impact**

- development of sport/leisure districts
- the introduction of new architectural styles
- the intrusion of conspicuous structures – architectural pollution
- preservation of green/open spaces – urban parks, golf courses, playing fields and so on
- eyesores caused by vast car parks

3 **Infrastructure**

- potential overloading of the existing infrastructure, particularly the transport network and public utilities
- the provision of new infrastructure – roads, car parks and so on
- additional urban management measures to adapt areas/buildings for leisure use

4 **Urban form**

- changes to the land-use pattern
- alterations to the urban fabric
- the use of brown-field sites
- a contribution to urban growth

Most of the popular sport and leisure activities have three things in common besides giving pleasure and entertainment and, as a result, contributing to our overall quality of life:

- They compete for urban space, which is a scarce and expensive resource. Also, they usually require purpose-built structures, which can make their mark – often a distinctive one – on the character of the built-up area (**4.4**).

- They generate traffic (vehicular and pedestrian) that converges on, and diverges from, the locations occupied by specific facilities (**4.4**).
- They attract people, and wherever people gather certain negative externalities seem to follow, such as noise, antisocial behaviour, litter, intrusive lighting and so on.

A curious paradox often becomes evident. Whilst many urban dwellers may wish for ready access to sport and leisure opportunities, that wish does not extend to literally living next to them. The reasons are largely contained in the last two of the above bullet points. It is better to live nearby rather than next door; that is, beyond the limit of the negative externalities.

Case study: Fear lurks in urban parks

The urban park is a vital, long-standing component of the urban sport and leisure environment. Traditionally, it has provided many opportunities, ranging from just sitting in a peaceful and green location or letting children play on swings and roundabouts to walking the dog or enjoying a relaxed game of tennis. It is estimated that urban parks are used on a frequent basis by 40 per cent of the UK population. But despite this, living next door to a park is not as cherished today as it used to be. The use of these parks nowadays is falling, but not through any deterioration in physical access. Rather, the parks are being blighted by fears and concerns about personal safety. Too many urban parks have become hotspots for a variety of crimes, such as taking and trading in drugs, mugging, rape, hooliganism and vandalism.

This case study serves to remind us that there is a two-way relationship between leisure and society. Leisure impacts on society, yes, but equally changes in society alter what we do in our leisure time and our use of leisure opportunities. Sadly, the opportunities of the urban park are as they have always been, but the prevalence of a more violent society means that they are increasingly under-used.

Review

7 Are you able to add to the list of impacts set out in **4.4**?

8 Explain the three typical locations of the fitness club (see case study on page 36).

9 Can you think of any more examples of changes in society impacting on leisure?

SECTION D

Impacts on the countryside

Whilst the majority of us live in urban environments, we frequently turn to the countryside for both sport (particularly in its play and welfare forms – see **Chapter 1 Section A**) and a wide range of leisure activities. What is the impact of this sport and leisure on the countryside, and are there any particular conflict issues? Of the sports that take place most commonly in the rural environments of MEDCs, golf and skiing are amongst the most popular. Mountain-biking is a relative newcomer, but is making its mark! Golf courses can be constructed in virtually any part of the world. Skiing, on the other hand, has some obvious physical needs (slopes and snow), the satisfaction of which means that its global distribution is somewhat patchy.

Over the last 25 years, global participation rates in golf have rocketed. Not just in MEDCs but also NICs, the demand for golf courses continues to escalate. The extent to which that demand is met varies considerably. For example, within the UK the provision of golf courses varies from one for every 12 000 people in Scotland to one for every 35 000 people in the South East of England. A review of the national situation in 1992 established that there was need for at least 700 more 18-hole courses. It also confirmed the mismatch between the patterns of supply and demand. Provision was claimed to be well below average in and around major urban areas. The problem here is that the unsuitability of most inner-city sites inevitably places the pressure on the rural–urban fringe and green-belt land.

Figure 4.5 The golf course balance sheet

Pros	Cons
There is a huge unsatisfied demand for extra golf courses	There is increased pressure on scarce land resources, particularly around major cities
Golf is a good use for damaged and degraded landscapes	Golf results in inappropriate use of areas of great landscape value
Golf courses contribute to much-needed agricultural diversification, particularly in marginal farming areas	There is a potential loss of top-grade farmland
A range of habitats can replace a previously rather sterile agricultural landscape	Ecology and wildlife may be damaged
Golf courses can conserve and enhance the countryside	Public access to the countryside is reduced
Golf courses are acknowledged as an alternative 'crop' in DEFRA's Set-Aside scheme	Damage is caused to heritage features, such as archaeological sites and historic parkland
Golf can coexist with other less formal countryside pursuits, such as walking and horse riding	The highly manicured artificial 'golfscape' is alien to the countryside
Planning applications for new courses must contain an environmental impact statement	The topography may be changed
Careful design can minimise visual intrusion	Golf 'furniture' (bunkers and paths) can be visually intrusive
Golf courses help to revive declining local economies by creating jobs, both directly and as part of a multiplier effect	There is a loss of peace and solitude, especially in remote unspoilt rural landscapes
Old farm buildings can be re-used as clubhouses	More traffic is generated
Golf courses enhance existing recreational opportunities	The 'thin end of the wedge' argument – further developments will follow
Golf courses enhance the value of rural land	Golf courses generate pressure on scarce resources such as water
The promotion of 'pay-as-you-play' courses can reduce golf's élitist nature	Golf courses introduce an élitist sport, often into relatively poor areas

Case study: The costs of Japan's love affair with golf

It would be remiss to talk about sport in Japan without mentioning golf. Japan is 'golf crazy'; it is one of the country's most popular leisure activities. In Japan, golf is a very expensive sport. Many cannot afford the high costs of club membership (often more than several years' salary) and have to be content with driving ranges and playing on pitch-and-putt courses.

Before the Second World War (1939–1945) there were only 23 golf courses in the whole of Japan. This number had risen to 72 by 1956. Now, there is a total of 1700 courses in operation, with another 330 under construction and roughly 1000 in various stages of planning.

Figure 4.6 High land costs are forcing Japanese golfers to play at higher altitudes and at increased environmental costs

Three-quarters of Japan is mountainous and largely forested. In recent years the construction of golf courses has turned to such areas. That it is better to build courses in the mountains than use the all too scarce coastal lowlands is proving to be a persuasive argument. However, golfing in the mountains comes with immense environmental costs. Course development requires clear-cutting forests, and the use of bulldozers to level hilltops and fill deep valleys (4.6). The mountain forests are important to Japan, not just for their timber, but also because they serve as a kind of natural dam, storing rainwater in the leaves and soil, and gradually releasing it into rivers and streams. In contrast, golf courses have only a quarter of the water retention capacity of forested areas. Most rainwater simply runs off greens and fairways. This results in flooding downstream. Equally, in times of drought, the water flow to streams and rivers from golf courses drops to a dribble.

An 18-hole golf course requires three to four tons of various germicides, herbicides and pesticides every year to keep the greens and fairways healthy, to combat weeds and to kill insects. Some of these chemicals are carcinogenic, while others are known to cause human deformities and nerve damage. The chemicals readily enter the water system, causing downstream damage to agricultural crops and fish stocks. The application of chemicals by spraying also means that they contaminate the air breathed by golfers. Ironically, while golf has an image as a healthy sport, the reality – and not just in Japan – may be rather different.

Golf courses can also pollute the social environment. Golf course construction companies often use connections with local government officials and politicians to help persuade farmers and other landowners to sell their land. In exchange, the construction companies often arrange for 'helpful' local officials and politicians to gain club membership at bargain rates. Since club membership is an appreciating and transferable asset, they are able to sell later at a massive profit.

Given the insatiable demand for golf courses and the growing awareness of their environmental costs, the Japanese construction companies are now looking elsewhere in Asia to help satisfy the needs of 'golf-crazy' Japan. The outcome of this is, of course, that golf moves from sport and leisure and into tourism (**1.1** on page 4). The 'costs' of golf are thus 'exported' to other countries.

Case study: Weekend skiing

Winter sports tend to be regarded as a branch of tourism in the sense that people travel to distant mountain areas and stay there for days, and perhaps even weeks. In reality, because of road improvements and increased car ownership, many people are able to participate in winter sports on a day-trip basis. This is the case in the Alps. At weekends in

Figure 4.7 The growing impact of skiing

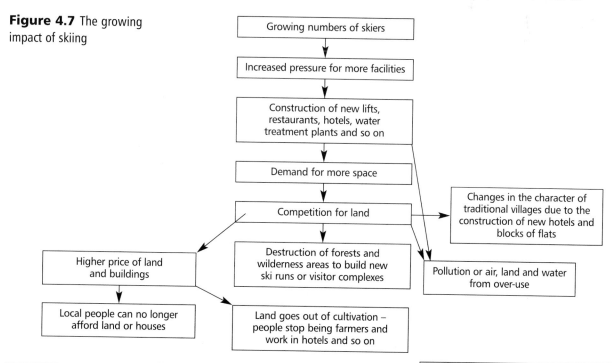

particular, people drive out of cities such as Geneva, Zurich and Salzburg and enjoy a day skiing in the mountains. In this case, skiing becomes a leisure activity rather than a tourist one. So, in the more accessible skiing areas, this activity is adding further to the general demand for more ski-runs and associated facilities. Some of the impacts of that demand are traced out in **4.7**. The overriding impression is one of costs – environmental, social and even economic. The question is: Does the leisure pleasure of those lucky skiers really justify the costs involved?

The compounding of leisure demands with those of tourism is also well illustrated nearer to home in the case of hill-walking, climbing and mountain-biking, particularly in areas such as the Pennines and the Lake District. Because of their accessibility from major cities, they have become well-established honey-pots for day-trippers. Day-trippers plus tourists means that at times, notably summer weekends and Bank Holidays, large areas of the countryside are literally overrun by thousands of visitors.

Case study: Mountain-biking

Mountain-biking has had a meteoric rise in popularity; so much so that it was included in the 2000 Olympic Games. Its appeal, particularly to urban dwellers, is based on the perception that it involves healthy exercise in pleasant surroundings. In some respects, the term 'mountain-biking' is misleading, in that this activity is not confined to upland areas. Indeed, mountain-bikers are to be found in large numbers in urban parks, along the country lanes, bridleways and footpaths of rural areas just beyond the urban fringe, as well as in distinctly lowland national parks such as the New Forest.

Mountain-biking has been the target of considerable criticism, largely because of its adverse environmental impacts, which include the trampling and erosion of soil and vegetation, the rutting and destabilising of slopes and the disturbance of birds and wild animals. It is generally placed well ahead of hiking in the damage league table and it is often ranked alongside horse riding. The density and volume of traffic are critical factors in the damage equation. Damage appears to be greatest in damp areas and during wet weather. It may be useful to confine mountain-biking to specified trails to protect some areas, but this merely concentrates the damage.

The negative externalities of mountain-biking are not confined to the physical environment. Studies have highlighted one major area of concern, particularly with respect to off-road activity. This is the **recreational conflict** generated with other leisure activities that use the same stretches of countryside and the same route ways. Walking and

Review

10 Check that you understand the reasoning behind the 'pros' and 'cons' set out in **4.5**.

11 Make a list of other sports and activities that qualify as components of both leisure and tourism.

12 Write a brief defence of mountain-biking as a leisure sport.

horse riding are the two most obvious examples. The view of some is that mountain-biking is an inappropriate activity in the countryside, and that mountain-bikers are not really interested in the environments through which they ride and which they disturb. The safety hazard created by mountain-bikers as they tear quietly along winding footpaths or through woodlands also contributes to the sense of conflict.

What is to be teased out of the case studies in this section (and that of the Glastonbury Festival in the previous one) is the considerable tension that exists between leisure activities and certain environments. The tensions are greatest in those areas that are most accessible from major cities. It tends to make a mockery of the idea of 'escaping' the city for peace, quiet and solitude. But maybe that is not what everyone wants. Perhaps some people are happy to remain part of the crowd. Nonetheless, at the end of the day how do we see the overall balance sheet – that is, between the social and psychological benefits reaped by individuals as they relax in the countryside and the costs of environmental damage, of conflict between different leisure activities and of the disruption of rural communities? On top of all this, what about the pollution caused by traffic as people travel between the city and the countryside in pursuit of sport and leisure?

SECTION E

Impacts on water environments

The list of water sports and water-based leisure activities continues to grow. We need to acknowledge that water, whether it is a stream or river, pond or lake, inshore or the deep sea, is a widely and increasingly used resource in the context of sport and leisure.

Case study: The Dorset coast

Attractive scenery is just one of the Dorset coast's resources that help to make it a honey-pot area for a whole range of sport and leisure activities. Other resources include its sandy beaches, its awesome cliffs, its sheltered stretches of water and its seabird colonies. What is becoming increasingly evident is conflict – not so much among the various recreational activities as between them and the environment. Some examples include:

■ the disturbance of cliff-nesting seabirds by climbers, air sports (for example, parascending) and the noise of water craft (for example, jet-skis and powerboats)

Characteristics	Class I Easily accessible	Class II Accessible	Class III Less accessible	Class IV Semi-remote	Class V Remote
Activities	Sunbathing People-watching Swimming Playing games Eating Skimboarding Sightseeing	Swimming Snorkeling Fishing Jet-skiing Non-powered boating Surfing Parascending Windsurfing	Usually boat-based Sailing Fishing Snorkeling/ scuba-diving	Some scuba-diving Submarining Powerboat (offshore equipped) Sailing – larger sailboats	Offshore sailing Live-aboard offshore fishing Remote coast sea-kayaking
Experience	Much social interaction with others High degree of services and support Usually crowded	Often contact with others	Some contact with others	Peace and quiet, close to nature Safety-rescue available Occasional contact with others	Solitude Tranquillity Closeness to nature Self-sufficiency
Environment	Many human influences and structures Lower-quality natural environment	Human structures/ influences visible and close by	Few human structures close by – some visible	Evidence of some human activity – for example, lights on shore, mooring buoys	Isolated High-quality Few human structures/ influences
Locations	Close to or in urban areas Beaches and intertidal areas	Intertidal → 100 m offshore	100 m → 1 km offshore	Isolated coasts 1–150 km offshore	Uninhabited coastal areas more than 50 km offshore

Figure 4.8 The spectrum of marine sport and leisure activities. Note that intensity of use and human impact decrease from left to right

- the disturbance of marine habits and their fauna by sub-aqua divers and the underwater noise generated by pleasure craft
- the erosion of cliff tops by so many people walking the coastal path
- the pollution, particularly of inshore waters, by discharges from yachts and launches
- the depletion of fish stocks by concentrated fishing at popular wreck marks and by beach angling.

Dorset's problems are by no means unique, but they perhaps exacerbated by the renowned beauty of its coastline and its accessibility from large centres of urban population, including London. Leisure is everyone's right, but what about the rights of the environment?

The so-called 'water sports' issue is not only the outcome of the increasing popularity of water sports. It also has to do with the increasing diversity of those activities. In the marine environment, five classes of activity may be recognised on the basis of the accessibility of the locations in which those activities typically take place (**4.8**). When it comes to dealing with the conflicts that they generate, there are four possible management strategies (**4.9**):

- **physical** – examples include site hardening (launching ramps, mooring buoys) and area sacrificing (designating particular areas for intensive use in order that other sites remain pristine)
- **regulatory** – examples include limiting visitor numbers, imposing speed limits, prohibiting certain activities and zoning for particular activities
- **economic** – examples include charging higher fees for certain activities, times or locations, imposing financial penalties for inappropriate/damaging behaviour and rewarding those who report such behaviour
- **education** – examples include distributing printed materials, displaying printed messages in appropriate locations and providing visitor centres.

Figure 4.9 Strategies to manage the recreational use of marine waters

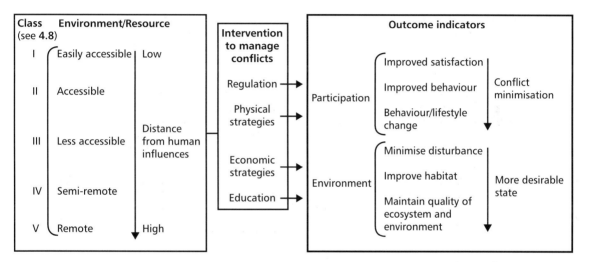

All four strategies can also be applied to inland waters. They seek to control participant behaviour and to protect or improve the environment. Physical and regulatory strategies are now widely applied, but to date the economic and education strategies have been focused on water-sport hotspots, such as Poole Harbour in Dorset and Windermere in the Lake District.

Case study: The ruffled waters of Lake Windermere

Windermere is the largest and most developed lake in the Lake District. Its eastern shore is a major focus of tourism and water-based sport. Ready access from large urban centres means that Windermere is far busier than any other lake. Figure **4.10** indicates the main negative externalities created by the high density of powerboats, jet- and water-skiers using the lake, particularly during warm summer weekends. In 1973 speed restrictions of 6 and 10 mph were imposed in particularly congested areas. Between then and 1991, there was a 300 per cent increase in powerboats capable of ever higher top speeds, many of which were towing water skiers; jet-skiers also began to appear. There was a commensurate rise in the negative externalities.

The Planning Policy Committee of the National Park decided that the time had come to take tough action and proposed that a 10 mph speed limit should be applied to the whole lake. This provoked a great deal of protest from fast water sports enthusiasts; they claimed that many local jobs would be lost as a consequence. Since then, the proposal has been the subject of a public inquiry, a judicial review and much prevarication on the part of the government. The 10 mph speed limit has now been made official, but will not come into operation until 2005. Figure **4.10** sets out some of the positive and negative impacts that may now be anticipated.

Figure 4.10 The impacts of imposing a speed limit on powerboats, jet- and water-skiers

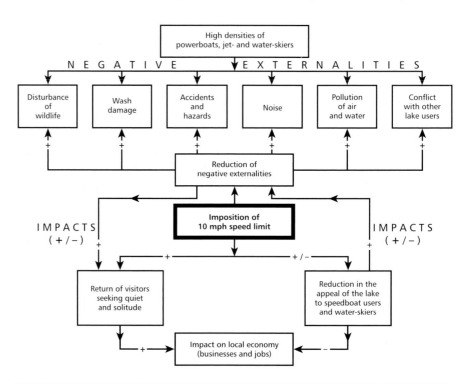

The point should also be made that the same broad strategies may equally be applied to sport and leisure on land, and indeed to sport and leisure in the urban environment.

This chapter has tried to explain and illustrate the sorts of impact that sport and leisure have on both people and places. The impacts come about in two main ways:

■ from provision of the facilities on which much sport and leisure depends
■ from the use of those facilities and from a general participation in sport and leisure.

In both instances, the outcomes involve a mix of costs and benefits, of negative and positive externalities. There are both down sides and up sides.

13 Draw a conflicts matrix for the sport and leisure activities of inland waters.

14 Do you think that the conflicts revealed in the Dorset case study can be resolved?

15 Assess the relative merits of the four different strategies outlined in **4.9**.

16 Check that you understand the reasons for the negative externalities shown in **4.10**.

17 Assume that you are a powerboat enthusiast. Set out your arguments in favour of removing the 10 mph speed limit.

Since the largest and densest populations occur in towns and cities, it is hardly surprising that it is here that the demand for sport and leisure is greatest. Whilst much of that demand is met within the urban environment, the impact inevitably spills over into the surrounding countryside. Gradients of declining demand, provision and impact are to be imagined as falling away with increasing distance from the urban fringe (see **3.11** on page 42). However, the consistency of those gradients is disrupted by the chance occurrence of a particular sport and leisure resource or opportunity. It might be a lake, the coast, a forest, a snow-covered slope or some purpose-built structure such as a marina, a picnic site, a ski lift or even a sports centre. Remember that, by definition, most sport and leisure is undertaken within the time frame of a day or less. For this reason, accessibility becomes an important factor that conditions the actual gradients of those slopes. Remember too that sport and leisure activities vary in their impact potential, and at the same time that environments vary in their sensitivity to sport and leisure use.

Enquiry

1 Research the management strategy adopted in one of the national parks in England and Wales to reduce the environmental impacts of leisure activities. Critically review the achievements of the strategy.

2 Investigate the distributions of two different leisure activities within a town or city known to you. Are the distributions different, and for what reasons?

3 Research the impacts of one sport or leisure activity on people, the economy and environment.

5

The globalisation of sport and leisure

An unstoppable force

Globalisation refers to those processes that increasingly override the national boundaries of the world. Although first and foremost an economic force, it does have important political and cultural dimensions. Many people argue that the globalisation of sport is an unstoppable process by which sports, participants, administrators and fans are subject to the forces of a global economy operating beyond the regulatory reach of nation–states. Manifestations of globalisation include:

- Manchester United's world tours, heralded by the simultaneous launch of new kit in Kowloon and Manchester
- polyglot rugby and football teams, trained by foreign coaches
- instantly recognised images on the world's billboards of megastars attired in Nike or Adidas gear
- world governing bodies controlling sport such as Formula One Grand Prix motor racing
- the worldwide sales at international airports of top team souvenirs.

A number of factors are encouraging this globalisation of sport and leisure:

- **The creation of international sports organisations**, such as the IOC (Olympics), FIFA (soccer) and the IAAF (athletics). They are highly powerful, due largely to the huge revenues that they derive from selling TV rights to Olympic, World Cup and World Championship events. They have the power to make or change the rules of sport and to bestow the right to hold mega-events.
- **Global telecommunications companies** increasingly control the scheduling, sponsorship and production of sporting competitions. As matches and races are beamed around the world, so a sense of the 'global village' is generated. This is sociocultural globalisation.
- **The internationalisation of teams, leagues and circuits for a global market** means that achievement sport has become global. This certainly applies to the international sports circuits, such as Formula One motor racing or Grand Slam tennis. The Brazilian national soccer team, Manchester United, the Harlem Globetrotters and the New Zealand All Blacks are among an élite of sports teams that have become **global brands**, known and respected around the world.
- **The new international division of labour** frequently leads to the production of sports equipment and apparel (sports shoes, footballs etc.) in poor Asian countries. This global shift to low-cost locations (see **5.8**) is

a classic example of TNC-led economic globalisation. The classic model is well shown by companies such as Adidas and Nike, with HQs and R&D facilities located in an MEDC, high-value goods produced in a NIC, and bulk production undertaken in LEDCs. Sports services also show the impact of globalisation. Sports management companies control 'stables' of sporting stars. Many leisure companies are also TNCs; they operate globally to deliver standardised leisure products.

■ **The global migration** of events, as well as of players, coaches and fans, is another facet of the globalisation of sport. As the volume of such movements increases, so hybrid, multicultural teams become the norm in most top-ranking football, basketball, rugby and cricket leagues. The stars of particular sporting circuits are the nomads of the modern world.

Figure **5.1**, which is derived from **1.4** on page 8, attempts to summarise the impact of globalisation on various levels of the sport and leisure industry. The remainder of the chapter explores these different impacts.

Review

1 Draw up a table to list the possible good and bad points about the globalisation of sport and leisure.

Figure 5.1 The globalisation of sport

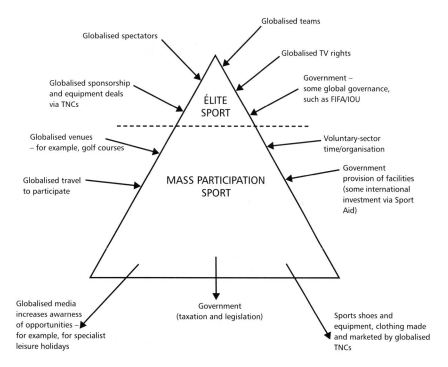

Globalised teams

Globalised spectators

Globalised TV rights

Globalised sponsorship and equipment deals via TNCs

Government – some global governance, such as FIFA/IOU

ÉLITE SPORT

Globalised venues – for example, golf courses

Voluntary-sector time/organisation

Globalised travel to participate

MASS PARTICIPATION SPORT

Government provision of facilities (some international investment via Sport Aid)

Globalised media increases awarness of opportunities – for example, for specialist leisure holidays

Government (taxation and legislation)

Sports shoes and equipment, clothing made and marketed by globalised TNCs

SECTION B

The anatomy of major global events

Major sporting events are of global significance. They involve competitors, spectators and viewers across the whole world, and generate hours of widespread media interest. They also have the potential to generate enormous amounts of economic activity and business for the host nation. Until the 1980s, hosting major sporting events, such as the Olympics, was thought to be a financial and administrative burden to both the organising city and the host country. For example, the Montreal Olympics (1976) lost £692 million and Munich (1972) £178 million. Admittedly, the latter was badly affected by terrorism. It was the 1984 Los Angeles Olympics that made the first surplus – £215 million. This financial success was based on blatant commercialism and large-scale sponsorship. The Los Angeles Games became known as 'the McDonald's games' and changed the way in which cities and their governments felt about hosting such great sporting events. Indeed, nowadays, cities and their national governments compete fiercely for the right to hold them (**5.2**).

Figure 5.2 Olympic Games locations and economic development

Ken Livingstone, the Mayor of London, said that he hoped to bring the 2012 Olympics to East London to revitalise the local economy. He said 'I believe East London has terrific potential to accommodate an Olympic stadium and village, with individual events taking place at other venues across London.' (*Daily Telegraph*, 14 July 2001)

Economic development was a large factor in Beijing's winning bid for the 2008 Olympics – China has only recently been allowed into the World Trade Organisation

The 1996 Olympics were held in Atlanta, USA, and were the first to be privately sponsored. Many firms were attracted to the area, which aided the city's existing gentrification and urban renewal schemes. The subsequent infrastructure improvements and migration to the city allowed the process of cumulative causation to occur

The Olympics in Tokyo and Seoul helped Japan and South Korea respectively improve their economies

Athens 2004 aims to reincarnate the original spirit of the Olympics and make Athens a top European city

After industrial decline in the 1970s and 1980s, Barcelona used the 1992 Olympics as a springboard to become one of Europe's leading cities

It has been estimated that the 200 Olympic Games in Sydney contributed about $6.5 billion to Australia's GDP

The first case study looks at a range of recent Summer Olympic events, all of which produced positive economic legacies. The second puts the spotlight on the most recent Winter Olympics, whilst the third is an early initial review of the 2002 World Cup. This last event seems to have bucked the trend and failed to hit the jackpot expected these days from the staging of a global championship.

Case study: Reaching beyond gold

A recent report bearing this title examined the legacies of four recent Olympics: Seoul 1988, Barcelona 1992, Atlanta 1996 and Sydney 2000. It also made forecasts about the profits to be expected from the Athens 2004 and the Beijing 2008 Olympic Games. It showed how host cities have learnt from the past and can now expect both short-term and long-term economic gains.

Figure 5.3 The short-term
economic impact of four
Olympic Games

Short-term gains

- The past four Summer Olympics generated considerable economic gains, mainly in the form of jobs and revenue (**5.3**).

Games	Permanent jobs	Estimated net economic impact (US$ billion)	GDP in year of games (US$ billion)	Economic impact as a percentage of GDP
Seoul 1988	55 000	2.6	182.0	1.4
Barcelona 1992	72 000	16.6	577.3	2.9
Atlanta 1996	78 000	5.1	7388.0	0.07
Sydney 2000	100 000	4.3	429.1	1.0

Long-term benefits

- **Urban regeneration** – each of the host cities capitalised on the games to revitalise run-down urban areas and regenerate brown-field sites. Barcelona was the beacon, but Atlanta probably brought about the most spectacular revival of an inner-city area, the Centennial Park area. In so doing, it combated both the doughnut effect and urban sprawl. The Sydney games were located on a site that had previously comprised an unusable swamp, a brickworks, a munitions dump and a meat packing house. In all cases, the Olympic villages that once housed competitors and officials have been re-used to make a positive contribution to each city's housing problems. Their design, location and form have also had dramatic long-term impacts on housing provision. The planned location of the village in Beijing will create a new focal point at the north end of the city. Infrastructure improvements are another major benefit for Olympic host cities. The games in Seoul led to an upgrade and expansion of Kimpo International Airport, new roads and underground stations. Athens has already built a much-needed new international airport, 120 km of new roads, expanded its metro system and commissioned a new ultra-modern traffic management centre.
- **Environmental benefits** – environmental issues are now a critical importance in the selection of a host city for the Olympics or a World Cup. By attempting to 'Green the games', Sydney has set standards for energy use, sustainable transport, waste disposal and environmental landscaping (see the case study on page 84). Athens aims to bring about a 35 per cent improvement in the quality of the environment (air pollution levels are a particular issue). Beijing has already set in motion a massive air improvement programme.
- **Promotion of tourism and the convention business** – the long-term payback to the host city in these two activities, and as a sporting venue, can be profound. Consider the case of Sydney, which transformed Australia, via the worldwide media, into a 'living postcard'. The 2000 Olympics were the biggest marketing event in Australia's history, with an estimated US $2 billion of free global publicity, not only for Sydney but for the whole of

Australia. In 2000, tourism arrivals in Australia were up by 11 per cent. In all four Olympic cities, convention business expanded by between 15 per cent (Seoul) and 34 per cent (Sydney) as facilities and hotels came on stream. Basically, progress in these businesses is all about re-imaging the city.

Successful hosting of the Olympic Games largely depends on the city concerned securing adequate sponsorship. This, together with government funding, is vital if world-class facilities are to be built. Management of the media is also necessary in order to promote attractive images and perceptions before and during the event, and to continue to deliver the dream afterwards. It is perhaps paradoxical that since the games are such 'cash cows', they have been held exclusively in MEDCs, with the exception of the 1972 Mexico Games. The mould is to be broken again by the 2008 Beijing Games.

Case study: A winter winner

The success story has at last reached the Winter Olympics too. A recent IOC report explains why the 2002 Winter Olympics staged in Salt Lake City, the capital of the Mormon State of Utah, were the most successful ever staged. The games generated enjoyment, huge viewing numbers, technical success, high-quality performances, financial profits with sponsorship and total ticket sales that broke all records. So how was this miracle brought about? The answer seems to lie in a judicious combination of:

- **sponsorship** – worth over $1000 million
- **licensing** – the 70 firms licensed to manufacture associated merchandise generated $500 million in revenue
- **ticketing** – 98 per cent of all tickets were sold, many on-line
- **technology** – 14 technology sponsors provided the best tested and most cost-effective and reliable solutions to timing, scoring, results and information diffusion services
- **broadcasting** – broadcasters reached 1.2 billion viewers in 160 countries
- **use of the Internet** – three million individual viewers logged on during the games, with an average number of 20 million page views per day; and many ticket applications were made on the Internet.

Subsequent questionnaires to participants and spectators provided very valuable and positive feedback.

Case study: Japan counts the real cost of co-hosting the 2002 World Cup

Japan spent over $4.5 billion on staging its part of soccer's World Cup in the summer of 2002. The money was spent mainly on infrastructure, such as stadiums, hotels, transport links and telecommunications. This expenditure compared with a figure of $1.5 billion spent by France when it hosted the event four years previously. The organising committee hoped that Japan would eventually recoup this investment. It also expected that it would break even on its operating budget of $437 million.

Hosting major sporting events is usually reckoned to bring a range of benefits. In this particular case, the following were anticipated in the short term:

- increased revenue from broadcasting rights
- raised revenues from advertising
- increased consumer spending – on national team kits, television sets, drink, trendy hairdressing and so on
- a boom in tourism, with full hotels and busy bars and restaurants
- a 'feel-good factor' that would distract attention from rising unemployment and other economic woes.

Figure 5.4 One of Japan's fine new stadiums – a white elephant?

In the longer term, there were hopes of:

- greater interest in and more support for Japanese football
- more foreign investment in Japanese clubs and players
- improved international understanding.

At the same time, it was also widely recognised that hosting this event might have a down side. In this instance, there were two particular fears:

- that of importing foreign football hooliganism
- that the six new stadiums and the four refurbished ones (on which so much money had been spent) would subsequently be under-used and become giant white elephants (**5.4**).

In the event, the wave of hooliganism that the media had primed Japan to expect did not transpire. Indeed, FIFA even praised the English fans for their exemplary behaviour.

Equally, the hoped-for economic benefits did not happen. Immigration officials had predicted that 337 000 supporters would travel to Japan for the World Cup. In fact, only 30 000 did: 12 000 of them were British, followed by 9000 Mexicans and 4000 Irish. The Japanese government has since admitted that the effect of the World Cup on the economy was, if anything, negative. This was partly attributed to the fact that people (both in Japan and elsewhere) stayed at home to watch the matches on TV. However, surveys do show that the event improved Japan's relations with South Korea (its co-host) and encouraged 'deeper friendly feelings' towards other countries, particularly England. This apart, the main beneficiary of the 2002 event was FIFA, which is estimated to have made over $700 million from media rights and merchandising.

Review

2 Having considered the Olympic and World Cup case studies, prepare a dossier of advice for future event hosts, such as Germany for the 2006 World Cup and Beijing for the 2008 Olympics.

3 What do you think are the key reasons for the failure of the 2002 World Cup to be an economic success?

Is the conclusion to be drawn from these three case studies that the Olympics are quite different from all other global championships, such as the World Cup? There are now world championships in about 20 sports. Each is tightly focused and appeals to a clear niche market. In these respects, they are not too different from the Winter Olympics. If that is so, then why are they not producing more revenue, sponsorship and spectators? In contrast, the Summer Olympics are a gargantuan event involving a wide but loosely related amalgam of sports. They are rather more like a fair or festival; for millions, the opening and closing ceremonies are the highlights. So are we to conclude from this World Cup and Olympics comparison that FIFA is much less efficient in its organisation and branding of a global event, or is it just the nature of the beast?

SECTION C

The global village

In the context of sport and leisure, the term **global village** refers to worldwide, mass participation in global events, such as the most recent World Cup, which was watched by up to 1 in 15 of all the world's people. More countries (204) are members of FIFA than are members of the United Nations (189). Football is the game that is always cited as most representative of the ideal of the global village. It is a game played and watched throughout the world, from the shanty towns of South America to the public schools of the UK. It is football – followed by basketball and baseball – that has led to the global branding of kit and equipment. Manchester United shirts (see **2.10** on page 22) and Nike trainers are the epitome of this. The global village of sport and leisure has been largely generated by the power of the modern media, particularly TV. Coverage of matches can now be beamed around the world, thanks to satellites, global communication via the Internet, mobile phone technology and the annihilation of distance by global transport systems.

Figure **5.5** illustrates the evolution of six different 'species' of football from a common root in the early 19th century. In terms of creating global villages, it is Association Football that has clearly led the way, perhaps followed by, in

Figure 5.5 The evolution and globalisation of football

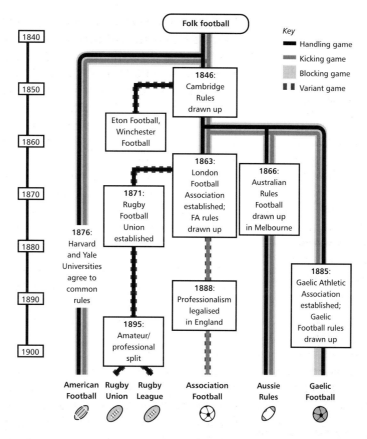

Review

4 a In your own words, explain what is meant by the **global village**.

 b Take one of the sport or leisure activities mentioned in the last paragraph and assess the degree to which it creates a global village.

order, Rugby Union, American Football and Rugby League. Aussie Rules and Gaelic Football remain parochial in the strictest sense of the word.

Are there other sport and leisure activities with the capacity to generate a global village? Basketball, rugby and even cricket are said to have some potential; after all, cricket has now even spread to isolated Bhutan! In terms of leisure, many would argue that the pop music global village is already well established, while some other activities, such as gambling and gaming, also have this potential – particularly since the English language is the dominant vehicle of communication.

SECTION D

International sport and leisure circuits

A number of sports, such as golf, tennis and athletics, have a fiercely negotiated annual calendar of major events that are literally spread around the world. Equally, there are some aspects of leisure that also have their global circuits; rock and pop festivals would be one such example. In this section, we will take a closer look at just one of the global sports circuits – Formula One Grand Prix motor racing. Hopefully, it will serve to draw attention to specific characteristics shared by the circuits of other sports.

Formula One (F1) motor racing can be said to have the greatest global media impact. The 17 Grand Prix events in a season have an immense exposure on global TV. According to the F1A (the governing body of the sport) the circuit of races in 2000 was watched by over 58 billion TV viewers in over 200 countries. It is reckoned that each F1 race attracts around 200 000 spectators and that over 3 million people attend during the course of the racing season (**5.6**). All of this means that F1 motor racing is one of the world's 'most watched' sports.

The migration of racing teams, drivers and equipment is matched by the migration of an enormous range of support personnel. The 'media circus' just for the printed Press consists of nearly 700 journalists and photographers from over 60 countries, all of whom travel the circuit. The 17 venues vary slightly from year to year; over 50 years F1 has visited 61 circuits in 24 countries, mainly MEDCS. Very strict rules and standards on circuit safety apply, and must be fully complied with if a circuit is to be retained.

Figure 5.6 Racing around a Formula One circut

Many nations and localities are queuing up to host Grand Prix races, if only because they create large amounts of wealth, particularly in the local economy. F1 races are unusual amongst major professional sporting events in that there is a high 'non-local' component amongst the spectators. Thus the money spent by incomers is 'new' or 'outside' money. Significantly, much of that money is spent outside the racing facility, as for example in the host community's retail outlets on such things as food, beverages, accommodation and transport. Also adding to the economic bonanza is the fact that an F1 race is a multi-day event, with the racing teams and the media arriving several days before the race and spectators coming to watch two days of practice sessions.

Clearly, F1 motor racing is a highly lucrative sport, not only in terms of what it can do for a local economy, but also in terms of sponsorship and media coverage. The last of these can do much to raise the profile and

5 You have the task of recommending:

- the closure of two of the European Grand Prix race tracks, and

- the locations for two new ones.

What criteria would you use in both cases? Suggest locations.

enhance the image of the host location and nation. There is no doubt that the F1A is one of the richest sport governing bodies in the world. That wealth also gives it great power, particularly when it comes to choosing the racing tracks that will be used during any given season. One can well imagine that the backers of race circuits, as well as the representatives of local and national governments, are constantly petitioning the F1A. All parties are anxious to win a slice of the immense revenues and global media exposure.

Hopefully, this case study has emphasised three particularly important points, namely:

- the powerful economic multiplier associated with staging just one in an annual global circuit of events
- the benefits that can accrue to a country and its race location from exposure in the global media
- the great power wielded by the sport governing bodies.

SECTION E

The creation of a global brand

Given the power of modern media and marketing, leading clubs and teams in a range of sports (particularly soccer) are working to become global brands. In other words, they want to become household names around the world and to use success on the field to generate enormous wealth. Manchester United is leading the way amongst European soccer clubs. The following case study looks at its efforts to go global.

Case study: Manchester United goes global

Manchester United has always had a reputation for commercialism. The current chief executive makes no secret of the club's global commercial ambitions, to transform Manchester United from a business that in 1998 depended on the UK for 98 per cent of its turnover to one with truly global income streams. In particular, the aim is to realise the potential of the North American and Far Eastern markets, with China as the long-term major prize. The target is 50 million fans worldwide.

The strategy is a very simple, but integrated, one. Its components include:

- a greater merchandising of replica kit and other paraphernalia, from mugs and mouse mats to shirts and signed photos

Review

6 Research one of the other emerging global sports brands: the All Blacks rugby team, Arsenal or Barcelona FC, the Brazilian soccer team and so on.

- the creation of new stores that combine space for selling club memorabilia with big screens for watching live matches, food and drink outlets and Internet access
- the forging of new-style sponsorship deals – the club has already signed deals with Nike (see case study on page 73) and Vodaphone worth nearly £350 million (see **2.10** on page 22)
- a more creative use of the media – there is already an MUTV subscription channel up and running
- using the club's Old Trafford HQ for a range of activities, guided tours, a superstore and a host of mega-events.

Remember, of course, that commercial success and winning on the pitch are closely linked. Winning matches fuels commercial success; equally, commercial success helps maintain the winning streak by allowing the club to bid for the best players.

SECTION F

The role of TNCs

Traditionally, TNCs are seen as one of the main instruments of globalisation: many of them have turnovers greater than the economies of many LEDCs. TNCs can be directly involved in the sport and leisure industry in a number of ways. These include:

- the marketing of global brands through the association of the brand with major athletics events, or using world sporting stars as 'clothes horses'
- the development of global service providers to support athletes and other performers
- the development of global service conglomerates to provide a huge range of leisure facilities
- the production of sports equipment and gear.

The making of a tennis ball used at Wimbledon provides a neat illustration of the last of these (**5.7**). Here, one could not wish for a better example of the globalisation of a manufacturing process.

Figure 5.7 The making of a Wimbledon tennis ball

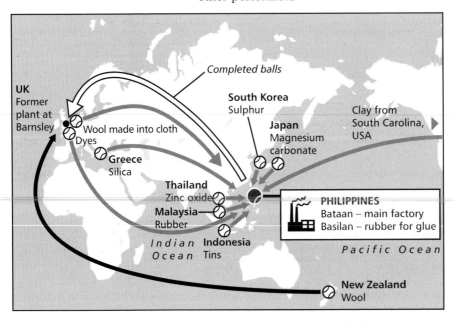

Case study: Nike's neat footwork

In terms of global TNCs, Nike is cited as the archetypal sports business. It has become the leading sports shoe producer and now accounts for 35 per cent of the market. Note the classic MEDC/LEDC 'formation' shown in **5.8**. Nike started out as a small company, called 'Blue Ribbon Sport' that was based in Oregon, USA (the current world HQ). Its business was the distribution of running shoes produced by Onitsuka, a Japanese company. In 1972, with a name change to Nike, the company began to design, make and market its own shoes. Although Nike has since moved into sportswear, shoes still constitute two-thirds of the company's business

Nike is not itself a manufacturing TNC. All of its manufacturing is undertaken by subcontractors, 99 per cent of it in Asia (**5.8**). Nike epitomises the 'don't stop moving' of the global shift as it is forever seeking the cheapest sites of production commensurate with maintaining quality. Wage cost rises in any location have to be offset by efficiency savings in production. Currently, Nike has a pool of around 40 main

Figure 5.8 Nike's global operations

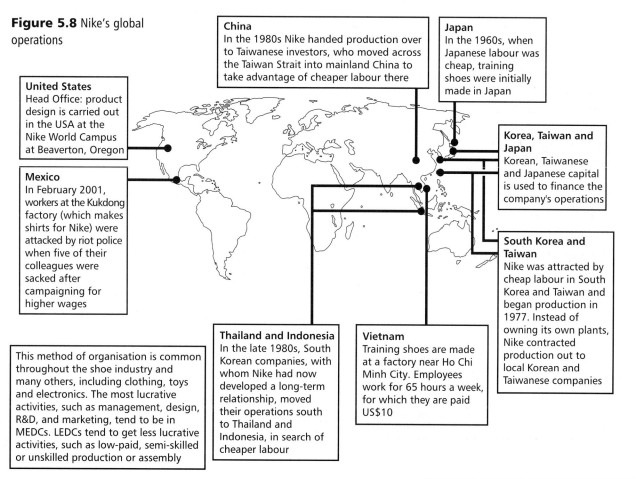

China
In the 1980s Nike handed production over to Taiwanese investors, who moved across the Taiwan Strait into mainland China to take advantage of cheaper labour there

Japan
In the 1960s, when Japanese labour was cheap, training shoes were initially made in Japan

United States
Head Office: product design is carried out in the USA at the Nike World Campus at Beaverton, Oregon

Korea, Taiwan and Japan
Korean, Taiwanese and Japanese capital is used to finance the company's operations

Mexico
In February 2001, workers at the Kukdong factory (which makes shirts for Nike) were attacked by riot police when five of their colleagues were sacked after campaigning for higher wages

South Korea and Taiwan
Nike was attracted by cheap labour in South Korea and Taiwan and began production in 1977. Instead of owning its own plants, Nike contracted production out to local Korean and Taiwanese companies

Thailand and Indonesia
In the late 1980s, South Korean companies, with whom Nike had now developed a long-term relationship, moved their operations south to Thailand and Indonesia, in search of cheaper labour

Vietnam
Training shoes are made at a factory near Ho Chi Minh City. Employees work for 65 hours a week, for which they are paid US$10

This method of organisation is common throughout the shoe industry and many others, including clothing, toys and electronics. The most lucrative activities, such as management, design, R&D, and marketing, tend to be in MEDCs. LEDCs tend to get less lucrative activities, such as low-paid, semi-skilled or unskilled production or assembly factories scattered around the globe, but in addition there are over 700 subcontracting plants in 50 countries to monitor. But the spatial pattern is constantly changing. In 1988, 68 per cent of Nike's shoes were produced in South Korea. Since then mass production has shifted to Thailand and Indonesia, and most recently to China, which now produces nearly 50 per cent of the output.

Global marketing is a key strategy for Nike. It does this by associating well-known athletes with particular Nike products. The athletes have to be talented, dedicated, highly visible and constantly in the news. Tiger Woods is a good example of such a sportsman. Nike spends around $1 billion annually on marketing and endorsement, in contrast to rivals such as Reebok, which spends less than 5 per cent of this amount and consequently loses business. Meanwhile Adidas, a German TNC, expanded in 1997 to become the second largest sports TNC, with global sales spread across sports shoes, clothing and equipment. It operates a similar organisational model to that of Nike.

A number of issues have emerged involving Nike and similar companies. Over the years, accusations have been made against them on the grounds of:

- using prison labour
- exploiting low-cost child labour
- running sweatshops
- harassing female workers
- not caring for the health and safety of workers.

To be identified with any of these practices is clearly potentially damaging to a company's image, and image is everything when it comes to pressing for sales. As a consequence, Nike, Adidas and others now pay considerable attention to monitoring the conduct of their subcontractors. They have also become actively involved in a range of campaigns and programmes designed to improve the conditions of their LEDC workers.

Review

7 Study **5.7** and assess the environmental and socio-economic impacts of the global shifts of production of Slazenger tennis balls.

8 Carry out further research into the costs and benefits for source and host countries of TNC control of sports goods manufacture.

Global migration in the sport and leisure industry

The migration of élite and potential élite sports talent is a marked feature of sports development over the last 30 years. Figure **5.9** shows how, even in the early days, a locational hotspot (see **Chapter 3 Section D**) developed from the movement of Rugby Union talent from South Wales to Rugby League in northern England. Sport and leisure labour migration occurs routinely within a country and between countries located within the same continent, but now is also evident at an intercontinental (or global) level. The flow volumes vary from sport to sport, with soccer, rugby and basketball arguably showing the greatest mobility.

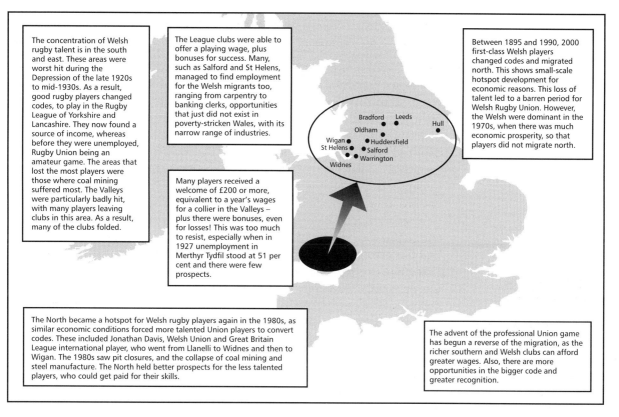

The concentration of Welsh rugby talent is in the south and east. These areas were worst hit during the Depression of the late 1920s to mid-1930s. As a result, good rugby players changed codes, to play in the Rugby League of Yorkshire and Lancashire. They now found a source of income, whereas before they were unemployed, Rugby Union being an amateur game. The areas that lost the most players were those where coal mining suffered most. The Valleys were particularly badly hit, with many players leaving clubs in this area. As a result, many of the clubs folded.

The League clubs were able to offer a playing wage, plus bonuses for success. Many, such as Salford and St Helens, managed to find employment for the Welsh migrants too, ranging from carpentry to banking clerks, opportunities that just did not exist in poverty-stricken Wales, with its narrow range of industries.

Between 1895 and 1990, 2000 first-class Welsh players changed codes and migrated north. This shows small-scale hotspot development for economic reasons. This loss of talent led to a barren period for Welsh Rugby Union. However, the Welsh were dominant in the 1970s, when there was much economic prosperity, so that players did not migrate north.

Bradford · Leeds ·
Oldham ·
Wigan · Huddersfield ·
St Helens · Salford
Widnes · Warrington
Hull ·

Many players received a welcome of £200 or more, equivalent to a year's wages for a collier in the Valleys – plus there were bonuses, even for losses! This was too much to resist, especially when in 1927 unemployment in Merthyr Tydfil stood at 51 per cent and there were few prospects.

The North became a hotspot for Welsh rugby players again in the 1980s, as similar economic conditions forced more talented Union players to convert codes. These included Jonathan Davis, Welsh Union and Great Britain League international player, who went from Llanelli to Widnes and then to Wigan. The 1980s saw pit closures, and the collapse of coal mining and steel manufacture. The North held better prospects for the less talented players, who could get paid for their skills.

The advent of the professional Union game has begun a reverse of the migration, as the richer southern and Welsh clubs can afford greater wages. Also, there are more opportunities in the bigger code and greater recognition.

Figure 5.9 How migration helped to create a new locational hotspot: Rugby League and the Welsh connection

Globalisation has encouraged sports migration, largely due to:

- international organising agencies
- TNCs keen to sponsor sporting talent
- global forms of communication that transmit information about opportunities around the world.

Equally important has been the proliferation of global competitions, both for teams and individuals, as well as relaxed regulations that govern the movement of sporting talent, as indeed of tourists.

For an athlete to migrate, there has to be a matching of needs and expectations against the characteristics of the existing sporting environment. There may be issues of persecution or lack of opportunity (poor facilities, insufficient financial support or inadequate training). Against these push factors there is the powerful pull factor of opportunity, which global communications and global commerce readily promote these days. But the final choice may depend on a number of personal factors, such as chance meetings, culture, language and also cumulative knowledge and confidence from previous successful migratory ventures. The recurrent paths followed by sports people gradually allow us to distinguish both talent-surplus regions and talent-deficit regions – areas of departure and arrival. Clearly, Kenya emerges as an example of the former, but it is interesting to note how the character of its talent exporting has changed over the last 50 years (**5.10**).

The global pattern of sport migration shows strong flows across the North–South divide, particularly from Africa to Europe. Within Europe, there have been significant East to West flows, particularly following the demise of the communist world around 1990. What we witness is sports talent from deprived or disadvantaged areas seizing the opportunity to earn lifetime security from valuable contracts and prizes. Most of these migrations are semi-permanent, because they are tied to fixed-term contracts. For these reasons, they are therefore subject to immigration and visa regulations. Short-term seasonal migration is also evident, particularly in sports such as cricket and rugby, with players playing (and earning) the year round. It has to be said that this practice is often to the detriment of health and fitness. The Grand Prix athletics circuit and the World Cup ski circuit are amongst those events that encourage temporary circulation at a global scale. In top-flight tennis and golf, players are essentially nomadic, as they move from tournament to tournament. Yet other élite performers and teams set up temporary training camps in warm weather or high-altitude locations to improve training, as for example in Lanzarote, Cyprus, Mexico or South Australia.

There are a number of issues that result from these global migrations. The movement of sports talent can in some cases de-skill and downgrade donor countries. For example, LEDCs and their teams make investments in nurturing sporting talent, and then as it reaches maturity MEDCs cream off the best players. Home audiences are thereby denied the chance to enjoy this home-based talent. The African exodus of football players from countries such as Senegal and Nigeria has had this effect. National teams can also be depleted of talent, if their new owners refuse to release them to

Figure 5.10 The outward movement of sporting talent from Kenya, 1950–2000

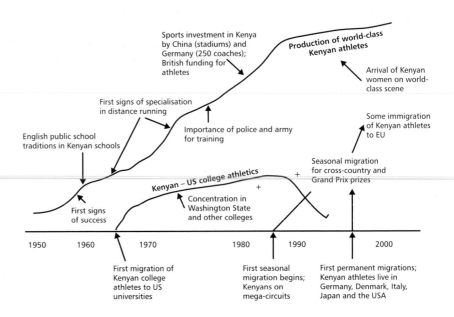

play for their country or they get injured. The plus side is, of course, the remittances, which are sent back home to the donor country.

Host clubs and host countries clearly gain much from importing sporting talent. They promise larger gates and higher revenues. Nonetheless, there are mixed views in England, for example, about the flooding of the Premiership with foreign soccer talent. There are relatively few English players turning out for the leading clubs these days. Some claim that this has reduced the opportunities for young home-based talent to develop and could lead to a crisis for the national team. On the other hand, spectators can watch an extremely exciting and beautiful game played by multi-skilled talent drawn from all corners of the globe. Inevitably, this globalisation can raise the sensitive issue of national identity, with some sports stars evolving into little more than mercenaries, seeking the highest bidder. Just think of the many European tennis stars who have become US citizens.

A final and obvious point to note is that the movement of spectators and fans to watch global sporting events and to support their teams helps to swell the volume of migration. Then just think of the immense flows generated by a whole range of leisure activities, and that pass collectively under the general heading of tourism (see Warn, 1999). For example, there are those who travel to participate in activity holidays such as scuba-diving or bird-watching in exotic locations. Here the role of low-cost global transport cannot be overemphasised. It now means that all those with money are able to pursue all manner of different sport and leisure activities almost literally anywhere in the world.

This chapter has been about the impact of globalisation, particularly on sport. Attention has focused on six different manifestations. In all of them it is possible to discern the hand of transport and communication. Advances in these fields are breaking down the barrier effects of national boundaries and distance, and in so doing they move us closer to the global village. Driving these advances is the much broader process of economic development. No matter where we live in the world, for most of us it is also delivering, to varying degrees, both the time and the means to enjoy worldwide sport and leisure.

Review

9   Write an analysis of the migration patterns shown by 5.13.

10 Identify the main problems resulting from global sports migration.

Enquiry

At the end of this chapter you should be able to write a report on:

■   the impact of globalisation on the sport and leisure industry
■   the role of TNCs in the sports business
■   the complex patterns of global sport and leisure migration.

CHAPTER 6

Challenges in the new millennium

In this last chapter, we look to the future. As far as sport and leisure are concerned, a number of broad hopes may be expressed. For example, most of us would wish that:

- the amount of leisure time continues to increase
- the choice of things to do in that time continues to broaden
- the present disparities in sport and leisure, as between MEDCs and LEDCs and between rich and poor people in all countries, will be reduced.

Perhaps the global slogan for the 21st century should be 'sport and leisure for all'!

However, pause for a moment. Think of the likely outcomes of these three praiseworthy aims. First, they will increase the overall demand for sport and leisure. This will put even more pressure on existing resources and facilities, many of which are already overstretched. This will also warrant the creation of new opportunities and the provision of new facilities, and will very likely do so in hitherto 'untouched' wilderness environments. Thus, straightaway, we begin to define a third challenge, namely to minimise or reduce to acceptable levels the adverse or negative impacts of providing for tomorrow's sport and leisure demands.

Figure **6.1** suggests that these future hopes just outlined are closely interrelated. Interestingly, they also provided the three dimensions in **1.3** (see page 6). Not only this, but they set out three vital directions from which to approach what we might call a more equitable and sustainable future – that is, providing sport and leisure for all, but in such a way that does not prevent future generations from meeting their sport and leisure needs. The next three sections look at each of these three pathways. They might also be seen as three specific challenges for the new millennium. They all have a clear geographical content.

Figure 6.1 Towards an equitable and sustainable future

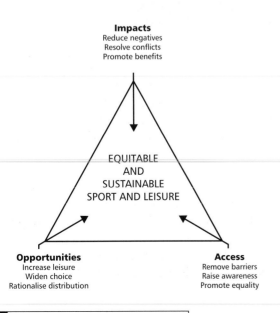

Impacts
Reduce negatives
Resolve conflicts
Promote benefits

EQUITABLE
AND
SUSTAINABLE
SPORT AND LEISURE

Opportunities
Increase leisure
Widen choice
Rationalise distribution

Access
Remove barriers
Raise awareness
Promote equality

Creating opportunities

The point was made in **Chapter 2** that sport and leisure is one of the many strands of the development process. The expectation is that development opens up sport and leisure opportunities, and that for most people delivery of those opportunities contributes to the general quality of life. We hardly need reminding of the great disparities in development that prevail in today's world, both between countries and within countries. Presumably these disparities trickle down into the world of sport and leisure. It would be absurd to suggest that the main reason for narrowing these development gaps should be to ensure 'sport and leisure for all'. However, the 'feel-good factor' generated by sport and leisure is widely acknowledged and is of such potential that few governments can afford to ignore it. Indeed, that is the key point. It is the responsibility of governments (national, regional and local) both to create sport and leisure opportunities, largely through provision, and to ensure their equitable distribution. The role of government should be one of planning and funding through taxation. Most would argue that it should also be to involve the private sector, as for example in the construction and running of facilities or through sponsorship.

Although funding is the main issue confronting governments, there is much that can be done (i) by curtailing the working week and ensuring that working people have time for sport and leisure, and (ii) though education. Education opens eyes, so in the present context it can help in making people more aware of sport and leisure opportunities and the personal benefits to be gained from participation. The next case study serves to illustrate this point.

Case study: War is declared on the 'couch potato' culture

In December 2002, the government launched a 20-year strategy to combat the 'couch potato' culture that is rampant in a sedentary, overweight and screen-fixated British society. People who are inactive are at greater risk of becoming obese and of developing, amongst other things, coronary heart disease, high blood pressure, diabetes and osteoporosis. It is claimed that inactivity is currently contributing to some 54 000 premature deaths a year, at a cost of £2 billion to the taxpayer in health spending. Sport has an important role to play in keeping people fit and healthy. However, the UK has a woeful record on keeping fit when compared with other European countries. Bad habits start young. Nowadays only 15 per cent of children walk to school, and when they get home they watch nearly four hours of television a day. Sport in the school curriculum has collapsed, playing fields are being sold off to developers and the UK has the sharpest post-school fall in sport participation.

1 To what extent do you agree with the view that, when it comes to distributing lottery money, sport and leisure should be a priority?

2 Why is education so important to the promotion of sport, leisure and health?

3 Write a brief critical review of the sports strategy outlined by the UK government in 2002.

The strategy put forward by the government involves a mix of targets and strands:

- ensuring that 75 per cent of children receive two hours' exercise a week at school by 2006
- encouraging at least 70 per cent of people to indulge in reasonable levels of exercise – about 30 minutes, 5 times a week – such as walking, gardening or cleaning the car
- setting up mobile gyms to encourage sport and fitness in deprived areas
- raising performance in élite sports by following the Australian model
- setting priorities for sports funding, with high-profile sports, such as football, rugby, cricket and tennis, receiving more money because their popularity creates a bigger public 'feel-good factor'.
- adopting a more cautious approach to the bidding for and hosting of major international sporting events.

If one had to criticise the strategy, it would be because of its heavy emphasis on competitive sport. Sport is not for everyone. The war on the 'couch potato' culture is more likely to be won by persuading people of the benefits of a more active use of leisure time. Walking, cycling, gardening, gentle jogging, bird-watching and regular visits to a fitness gym are amongst the most effective armaments to deploy in winning the war.

SECTION B

Improving access

The challenge of creating opportunities is closely tied up with that of improving access. For example, the question of whether or not the spatial distribution of sport and leisure opportunities is an equitable one hinges on their physical accessibility. Are the transport systems and networks such that, no matter where they live, people have a reasonably equal chance of reaching those opportunities, should they so wish? Without belittling the significance of transport, it needs to be stressed that the concept of access is altogether much broader. The examination of participation rates in **Chapter 3** clearly showed considerable differences between social and ethnic groups, as well as on the basis of gender and age. Yes, these are important dimensions of the whole access issue. Their geography lies in the fact that they vary from place to place.

Access has two faces – inclusion and exclusion. When it comes to sport and leisure, the key influences on both faces of access include disposable income, levels of educational attainment, occupational status, social class, culture and ethnicity, gender, age, ability and disability. The challenge is to promote the former and reduce the latter. With exclusion, it is more helpful to think in terms of dismantling barriers to participation.

Reference has already been made to one physical barrier – the poor or unfair location of facilities. Another obvious example is poor levels of

Main groupings	Specific barriers
Physical	Uneven provision relative to demand Low levels of personal mobility Physical handicap
Cultural	Values Codes of conduct Customs
Ethnic	Discrimination against minorities Perceptions Segregation
Economic	Disposable income Long working hours Occupational status Cost
Political	Lack of representation Alienation Government policy and priorities
Social	Social class Gender Age and stage in the life cycle Occupational status

Figure 6.2 Some barriers to participation in sport and leisure

personal mobility. Economic barriers relate to affordability, cost and the perceived value of that cost. Cultural barriers include the direct conflict between cultural values and the codes, customs and convention of particular activities. For example, for many Islamic women there are deep-seated conflicts associated with participating in leisure activities outside the home, particularly in mixed-sex groups. Then again, cultures differ in terms of the importance attached to sport and of what they would see as appropriate and attractive leisure activities. Political barriers to participation relate to feelings of having little choice or little involvement in the decision-making processes of sport and leisure provision. The barriers are alienation and the perception of being in some way disenfranchised.

Social barriers to participation include class, age and gender. Sport fishing shows strong signs of social polarisation and the existence of a class-barrier effect. Whilst the working class coarse-fishes in public ponds and inshore waters, the aristocracy and wealthy fly-fish along carefully guarded rivers, for salmon in the Scottish Highlands or for trout in the Chalk streams of southern England. It is an inescapable fact that age will always be something of a barrier, if only because the ageing process reduces physical capabilities and changes leisure interests. However, in a society in which people are living longer, there is increasing awareness of the benefits that healthy and active leisure can bring. Even so, there is still considerable scope for promoting this belief and for ensuring that people are not debarred from doing things that they wish to on the grounds that they are too old. Figure 6.3 shows how participation in individual and team sports has influenced the four social factors of gender, age, stage in the life cycle and type of household.

Without wishing to sound complacent, great strides have been made in MEDCs to reduce the gender barriers that once prevailed in sport and leisure. Nowadays, few would argue that the sexes have different roles to play in society or that sport is only for men (the claimed 'stronger' sex). Women today not only participate in sports, such as football, rugby and cricket, that not so long ago were regarded as male preserves, but performance standards have risen enormously and the gender gap has been significantly reduced. Women have joined the ranks of sports professionals, organisers, media commentators and personalities. Perhaps sitting rather uneasily with notions of equal opportunities is the large number of international sporting organisations and competitions that are

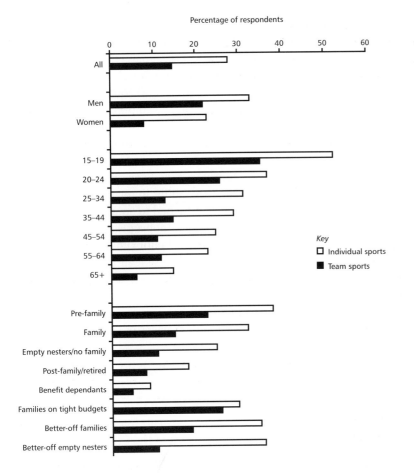

Percentage of respondents

Key
□ Individual sports
■ Team sports

Figure 6.3 Participation in individual and team sports by sex, age, stage in the life cycle and type of household

exclusively for women or men. Does separatism really help to remove barriers? Surely, integration and mixed sport offer a more promising way forward!

Overcoming the barriers to participation involves developing strategies that challenge the inequitable nature of existing provision. There are real limitations to what can be achieved within sport and leisure. Many of the barriers there have their roots in broader processes, and in institutions and structures that are firmly embedded in society. If the barriers to participation are physical, economic, cultural, political and social, then so too are any possible solutions. But we should understand that legislation in any or all of these fields can only do so much. If nothing else, changing hearts, minds and traditions requires an abundance of time and a liberal helping of education.

Case study: Stoke-on-Trent targets the young

Stoke-on-Trent has already figured as a case study in **Chapter 3**. We now revisit the city to look at its Sports Action Zone (SAZ) strategy to ensure that 'all young people,' up to the age of 25, 'have the opportunity to enjoy the benefits of sport and active recreation, irrespective of their personal circumstances, for example who they are or where they live'.

Poor physical and mental health is closely correlated with other measures of deprivation. Research in Stoke has revealed that poor health among people under the age of 25 is linked to:

■ poor nutrition
■ low levels of physical activity
■ high levels of childhood obesity

- high levels of teenage pregnancy
- high incidence of smoking, alcohol intake and substance misuse
- high levels of being unable to cope, especially among girls
- low levels of self-esteem, confidence and aspiration.

Many young people in Stoke claimed they were excluded from sport and active leisure pursuits for various reasons. These included ethnicity, sexual inclination, disability, homelessness, unemployment and having a criminal record.

So the challenge facing the SAZ was how best to remove this sense of exclusion (perceived and real). The answer was thought to lie not so much in providing more facilities but, rather, in:

- increasing awareness amongst the SAZ target groups of the personal benefits of participating in sport and active leisure
- improving communications between sport and leisure providers and the target youth groups
- building up partnerships between the various organisations (including schools) concerned with young people and the reduction of deprivation.

Perhaps most crucial of all is the need for early intervention if the cycle of disengagement experienced by socially excluded youngsters is to be broken.

Review

4 Can you think of any more barriers that might be added to those listed in **6.2**?

5 What conclusions do you draw from an analysis of **6.3**?

6 In your own words, describe the causes and outcomes of the 'cycle of disengagement' referred to in the Stoke-on-Trent case study.

7 This section has been largely about removing exclusion and the barriers to participation. Does promoting the inclusive side of access necessarily involve the same actions?

SECTION C

Reducing impacts

'Sustainability' is one of today's buzzwords. It hinges on the idea of meeting our present needs without compromising the ability of future generations to do the same. The two previous sections and much of **Chapter 4** have made the point that sport and leisure developments pose increasing environmental threats and therefore, by implication, are unsustainable. But sustainability is about more than just protecting the environment. It is to do with the careful use of scarce, often non-renewable, resources. In the present context, it is also about reducing the sorts of negative externalities that were discussed in **Chapter 4**. That is a pleasant thought, but is it really feasible to provide for sport and increasing leisure in a sustainable way? An answer will be sought in two different situations that really mark the ends of the sport and leisure spectrum – the mega-sports event and the more individual, day-to-day leisure activity of mountain-biking!

Case study: The 2000 Sydney 'Green' Olympic Games

Sustainability was given a high profile in the preparation for and running of the Sydney Olympic Games. Subsequent evaluations by various organisations, such as Greenpeace and the National Geographic Society, yielded a balance sheet of 'wins' and 'losses' with respect to the environment (**6.4**).

Figure 6.4 The environmental balance sheet of the Sydney Olympics

'Wins'	'Losses'
The high-quality development of a derelict brown-field site	Major sponsors, such as Coca Cola and Samsung, failed to comply with the 'Green' policies laid down by the organising committee
The use of solar power for the lighting of the Olympic village, the Stadium, the Plaza and other venues	The village built for the world's media personnel was not solar-powered as originally planned
Village furniture made from recycled cardboard	Nothing was done to reduce the toxin levels of nearby waterways
Non-toxic paint, PVC-free pipes and plantation timber used in venue construction	Some building materials involved PVC plastics and non-renewable timber
The use of electric- and gas-powered public transport in the movement of competitors and spectators	HFCs and CFCs in air-conditioning units and refrigerators
The designation of car-free areas	Increased aviation fuel consumption and CO_2 emissions due to increased international flights to and from Sydney
The adoption of a integrated waste management and recycling strategy	

Thanks to modern communications technology, large-scale sporting events have raised profiles. They are ever more open to scrutiny by a public that is increasingly alive to sustainability issues. Whilst that certainly encourages the planning of moves in the right direction, the Sydney case study suggests that actions are falling well short of true sustainability. Is the record any better for the more run-of-the-mill, everyday forms of sporting leisure? Take the case of mountain-biking that was discussed in **Chapter 4**. Whilst potential environmental impacts may be limited (not completely avoided) by constructing purpose-built trails and confining cycling to them and to roads, it only takes a few perverse individuals to decide to ride off trail and sustainability is immediately threatened.

The Sydney Olympics case study and the example of mountain-biking both underline the need for education. It needs to be understood that sustainability depends not on rhetoric and gestures, but on unwavering commitment and coordinated actions. Sustainability is quickly compromised by lapses and steps out of line, no matter how small. The commercial interests that permeate such much of today's sport and leisure represent another stumbling block. In Sydney, a number of TNCs seemed to think, perhaps because they had had done so much by way of sponsorship, they should be excused from observing the 'Green' guidelines specified by the organising committee. With mountain-biking, manufacturers need to promote the sale of bikes, clothing and safety gear, and often do so on the basis that their products perform best under extreme conditions – in other words, under those conditions when environmental damage is likely to be greatest.

The broad conclusions to be drawn from the discussions in this and the two previous sections may be summarised as follows:

- development is generally expected to deliver more sport and leisure opportunities
- closing the development gap both between and within countries promises a more equitable distribution of those opportunities
- improving anything other than the physical accessibility of sport and leisure will require fundamental reforms to, and structural changes within, modern society
- much can be done to reduce the negative impacts of sport and leisure, but it remains to be seen whether sustainability is really attainable
- a damaging tension exists between globalisation, together with the commercial interests that infiltrate so much sport and leisure, and the general move towards sustainability
- governments have major responsibilities in all three pathways to a more equitable and sustainable sport and leisure.

Review

8 How successful do you think was the attempt to 'Green' the Sydney Olympics?

9 Explain why and how globalisation affects the sustainability of sport and leisure.

SECTION D

New technologies – new opportunities and threats?

An appropriate question to ask at the very end of this book is about the new technologies that are just appearing over the horizon. Will they significantly alter the rather disappointing conclusions just summarised? At best, we can only second-guess what lies in store. The immediate horizon seems to be dominated by the continuing ripples of the communications and information revolution. Today's CDs and DVDs already bring much leisure entertainment into the home; interactive TV is enhancing our experiences as sport spectators; and computer games and virtual reality are encouraging us to participate in all sorts of new 'sporting' challenges. The Internet allows us to reach out to an amazing world of information and entertainment. Indeed, there is a real prospect that tomorrow's sport and leisure activity will be even more home-based than today's. Given parallel moves such as armchair shopping, virtual reality travel and home-based working, perhaps the day is not too far off when leaving the home will be something that we do only on rare occasions. Clearly, such a scenario is only imminent in some MEDCs; the future for LEDCs may turn out to be a different one.

It is somewhat ironic that the impact of these moves towards a more home-based, computer-based lifestyle is likely to be on people rather than on the environment. Fair enough, production of the increasingly sophisticated hardware and software needed to deliver these new opportunities does have environmental costs. Production uses scarce and often non-renewable resources and generates pollution. However, just think about the potential human costs – the threat to human health of a lifestyle fixated on sitting in front of a computer screen in an artificial environment, or the threat to a society made up of people who are increasingly isolated, perhaps even alienated, in their homes. This would represent a major advance of the 'couch potato' culture. The best hope is that people will quickly realise that while fashions change, the quality of life is best enhanced by a diet of sport and leisure that mixes both active and inactive modes, as well as the best of the new and the tried and tested of the past.

Enquiry

1   Take a look in the crystal ball. What other new technological developments do you see as possibly having an impact on future sport and leisure? Present a brief report (verbal or written) and try as best as possible to support your answer with examples.

2   Having read this book, set out what you think are the main contributions that geography can make to the study of sport and leisure.

3   Explain and illustrate the two alternative approaches to future sport and leisure provision – the 'top-down, capital-intensive' and the 'bottom-up, community-based' models. Which do you think is likely to prove more sustainable? Give your reasons.

Further reading and resources

Some book references include the following:

J. Bale, *Sport, Space and the City* (Routledge, 1993)

J. Bale, *Sportscapes* (Geographical Association, 2000)

J. Bale, *Sports Geography* (Routledge, 2002)

J. Coakley, *Sport in Society* (McGraw-Hill, 2001)

T. Elvin, *Sport and Physical Recreation* (Longman, 1990)

C. Gratton and P. Taylor, *The Economics of Sport* (Spon Press, 2002)

C. Hall and S. Page, *The Geography of Tourism and Recreation* (Routledge, 2002)

HMSO, *The Environmental Impact of Leisure Activities* (1995)

B. Houlihan, *The Politics of Sports Development* (Routledge, 2001)

A. Mason, *Sport in Britain: a Social History* (Cambridge University Press, 1989)

Mintel (UK), *The Sports Market* (1991)

R. Prosser, *Leisure, Recreation and Tourism* (Collins, 2000)

I. Roberts, *Leisure and Recreation* (Heinemann, 2001)

S. Warn, *Recreation and Tourism: a Changing Industry* (Stanley Thornes, 1999)

S. Williams, *Recreation and the Urban Environment* (Routledge, 1995)

Useful periodicals include the following:

Countryside Focus (available free from the Countryside Agency)

Journal of Leisure Sciences

Journal of Sport and Social Issues

Leisure Studies

Sports Business

There are also many specialist popular magazines, including:

Biking

The Climber

The Diver

The Golfer

The Rambler

Ski-monthly

The Internet can be extremely helpful. The following list summarises websites used in the preparation of this book, and provides resources for the Enquiry task in **Chapter 3**:

http://www.countrysideagency.org.uk

http://www.lakedistrict.gov.uk

http://www.infoplease.com

http://www.wsgi.com

http://www.olympics.com

http://www.olympic.org

http://www.google.com

http://www.Beijing-2008.org

http://www.2002worldcupKorea.org

http://www.physicaleducationsports/participation.com

http://www.commonwealthgames.com/manchester/legacy

http://www.bbc.co.uk/sport

http://www.IOC.org

http://www.nps.gov